Stage Costumes
for Girls

Stage Costumes
for Girls

By

Jean Greenhowe

Publishers   PLAYS, INC.   *Boston*

© Jean Greenhowe 1975

First American edition published by Plays, Inc.
1976
Reprinted 1980
Published in Great Britain under the title
Fancy Dress for Girls

Library of Congress Cataloging in Publication Data

Greenhowe, Jean.
Stage costumes for girls.
British ed. published under title: *Fancy Dress for Girls*
Bibliography: p.
1. Children—Costume. 2. Sewing. I. Title.
TT562.G7   646.4′7   75-23205
ISBN 0-8238-0196-9

Printed in the United States of America

Contents

Acknowledgment

My sincere thanks are due to Victoria and Jacqueline who modelled the costumes for the photographs in this book.

Introduction

The following pages contain full instructions for making fourteen costumes for girls to fit any sizes up to about 147cm (4 ft 10-in.) in height. I have devised various methods by which all the garments can be constructed to fit any child's individual measurements without the need of complicated pattern pieces. Very simple basic shapes such as rectangles and circles are used for patterns and the only dressmaking experience required is to be able to gather, sew seams and turn hems.

By using these simple methods I hope the reader may be able to design and make other outfits. Some books on historical costume are listed in the bibliography and these can be referred to for further ideas.

Jean Greenhowe

General instructions

These should be read before starting to make any of the costumes.

Fabrics and other materials

For convenience the lists of materials required for each garment are given for height 147cm (4 ft 10-in.) but the costumes can also be made for even taller children. By reading through the instructions, the little extra amounts of fabric required for a taller child can be fairly easily calculated. In the same way, if a costume is to be made for a child smaller than 147cm any obvious savings which can be made, for example in the length of a garment, can be ascertained by first reading through the instructions.

The making up instructions are written in such a way that they cover all sizes at each stage of making so that the garments can be made to fit any child's individual measurements.

Curtain fabrics are especially good for making costumes since they are normally much wider than dress fabrics. Remnants of curtaining can also be bought quite cheaply in the sales. The non-woven type of curtain fabric is very useful because it is inexpensive, does not fray at the cut edges and can be obtained in a range of bright colours.

Velcro touch and close fastening is very good for waistband and other fastenings though hooks and eyes or snap fasteners can be used instead.

Stiff interlining is ideal for making hat and collar shapes and the stiffest kind of *Vilene* is best of all. This is normally used for interlining curtain pelmets and home furnishing in general and it is 82cm (32 in.) in width.

An old sheet, if available, will provide a valuable quantity of fabric for making such things as under-skirts and aprons.

Making the patterns

The pattern shapes should be drawn out to the measurements given on large sheets of brown wrapping paper or newspaper. A yard stick or long straight piece of wood will be found very useful for drawing straight lines. An ordinary compass should be used for drawing out small circles but for many of the garments, larged curved or circular patterns are required and these can be easily drawn out as follows. Fold a square of paper of sufficient size into quarters. Tie a pencil to one end of a length of string which should be longer than the required radius of the circle. Note that the radius of a circle is half the diameter. Measure the length of the radius along the string from the pencil and tie a knot in the string at this point. Place a drawing pin through the knot and in to the folded corner of the square of paper. Now draw out the quarter circle as shown in the diagram keeping the string tightly stretched. Cut out, then open up the folded sheet to give the full circle.

Sewing and glueing

Seams measuring 1·3cm ($\frac{1}{2}$ in.) are allowed on all pieces unless otherwise stated. Press the seams open after sewing.

Join all pieces of fabric having the right sides together unless other instructions are given.

The raw edges of seams may be finished off if desired by oversewing. In some cases adhesive is quoted in the materials lists and this should be an all purpose clear adhesive such as *UHU* which is colour-less and dries very quickly.

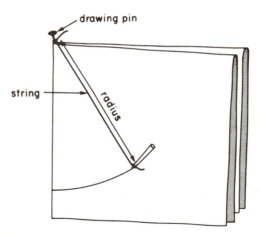

Drawing out large circles

Grecian costume, 5th century B.C.

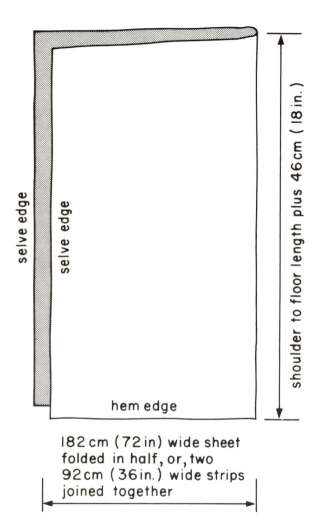

selve edge

selve edge

hem edge

shoulder to floor length plus 46cm (18 in.)

182 cm (72 in) wide sheet folded in half, or, two 92 cm (36 in.) wide strips joined together

1. *Folding the fabric in half*

The Doric chiton is made from a cotton sheet and requires very little sewing since it is simply a rectangular shape folded around the body. The head-dress, covered with gold fabric, is trimmed with thin gold cord for decoration.

Chiton

Materials required to fit any size.
A 182cm (72 in.) wide bed sheet, or, if fabric is bought by the yard two 92cm (36 in.) wide pieces the child's shoulder to floor length plus 46cm (18 in.).
3·7m (4 yd) of ribbon or braid for trimming the chiton.
1·9m (2 yd) bias binding.
70cm ($\frac{3}{4}$ yd) of narrow elastic.
2 gold buttons.

To make

Fold the fabric in half across the width as shown in diagram 1. If two 92cm (36 in.) wide pieces are used, join them together to make a 182cm (72 in.) wide piece. Fold the top edge over to hang down about 30·5cm (12 in.) as shown in diagram 2, noting that for small children the turnover will be smaller. This flap of fabric should be just above waist height as shown in the illustration.

Mark the points A and B on the top folded edges as shown in diagram 2, then lap the points A over points B and pin. Sew a button through all the layers of fabric at the pinned positions. Try the chiton on the child and mark on the position of the natural waist-line. Stitch bias binding to the inside of the chiton about 8cm (3 in.) below the waistline mark. Thread

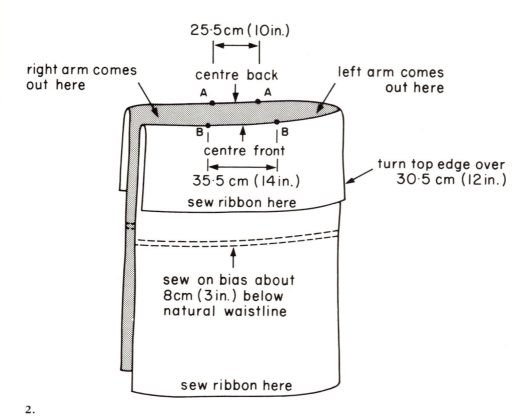

25·5cm (10in.)

right arm comes
out here

centre back

A   A

left arm comes
out here

B | | B

centre front

35·5 cm (14in.)

sew ribbon here

turn top edge over
30·5 cm (12in.)

sew on bias about
8cm (3in.) below
natural waistline

sew ribbon here

2.

elastic through the bias and knot the ends together to
fit the waist.

    Try the chiton on the child and cut off any excess
length if necessary to make it floor length. Hem, then
sew ribbon or braid to the lower edge and the folded
over piece as illustrated.

Head-dress

Materials required to fit any size.
Small pieces of stiff interlining or card, and fabric.
1·9m (2 yd) of thin gold cord.
92cm (1 yd) of 1·3cm ($\frac{1}{2}$ in.) wide ribbon.
Adhesive.

13

3. *The head-dress pattern*

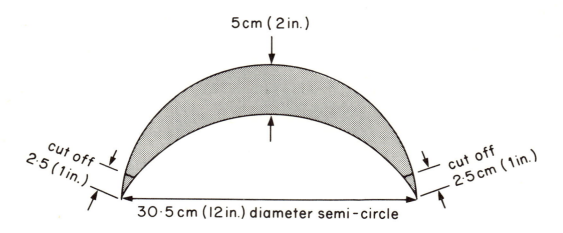

5cm (2in.)

cut off 2·5 (1in.)

cut off 2·5cm (1in.)

30·5cm (12in.) diameter semi-circle

To make

First make a pattern by drawing out a 30·5cm (12 in.) diameter semicircle. Draw another curve inside the semicircle as shown in diagram 3. Cut out the shape then cut about 2·5cm (1 in.) off the points at each side.

Cut the shape from interlining or card and stick fabric to each side of it, trimming the fabric even with the shape. Glue cord all round the shape at the edges then stick on lengths of cord to make designs as shown in the illustration. Attach 46cm ($\frac{1}{2}$ yd) of ribbon to each end of the head-dress.

Hair

If the hair is long gather it up in to a chignon at the back of the head. The head-dress is then tied round the back of the head taking the ends of the ribbon up around the chignon. Arrange short hair in little curls on the forehead.

Sandals

Plastic flip-flop sandals can be worn.

14

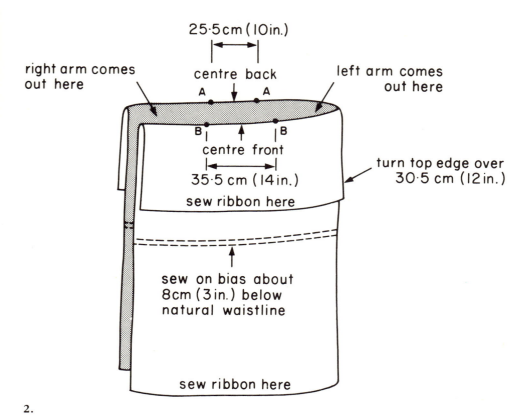

2.

elastic through the bias and knot the ends together to fit the waist.

Try the chiton on the child and cut off any excess length if necessary to make it floor length. Hem, then sew ribbon or braid to the lower edge and the folded over piece as illustrated.

Head-dress

Materials required to fit any size.
Small pieces of stiff interlining or card, and fabric.
1·9m (2 yd) of thin gold cord.
92cm (1 yd) of 1·3cm ($\frac{1}{2}$ in.) wide ribbon.
Adhesive.

3. *The head-dress pattern*

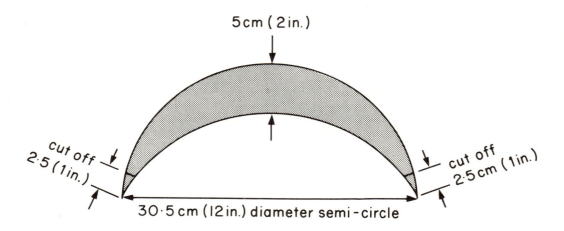

5 cm (2 in.)

cut off
2·5 (1 in.)

cut off
2·5 cm (1 in.)

30·5 cm (12 in.) diameter semi-circle

To make

First make a pattern by drawing out a 30·5cm (12 in.) diameter semicircle. Draw another curve inside the semicircle as shown in diagram 3. Cut out the shape then cut about 2·5cm (1 in.) off the points at each side.

Cut the shape from interlining or card and stick fabric to each side of it, trimming the fabric even with the shape. Glue cord all round the shape at the edges then stick on lengths of cord to make designs as shown in the illustration. Attach 46cm ($\frac{1}{2}$ yd) of ribbon to each end of the head-dress.

Hair

If the hair is long gather it up in to a chignon at the back of the head. The head-dress is then tied round the back of the head taking the ends of the ribbon up around the chignon. Arrange short hair in little curls on the forehead.

Sandals

Plastic flip-flop sandals can be worn.

Pedlar costume, 19th century

The pedlar illustrated carries in her basket a selection of modern goods and also some items of Victoriana. If a few such old bits and pieces are available they will add to the charm of the costume but they are not essential. Any kind of 'goods' can be offered for sale. For fund raising at a summer fête or charity bazaar children could be dressed as pedlars, selling home-made sweets, cakes, lavender bags, flower posies etc.

Blouse

Use an ordinary long sleeved blouse or sweater.

Skirt

Materials required for height 147cm (4 ft 10 in.).
1·9m (2 yd) of 92cm (36 in.) wide cotton fabric printed with a small design in dark colours.
Length of 2·5cm (1 in.) wide petersham ribbon to match the fabric, the child's waist measurement plus 5cm (2 in.) for an overlap.
5cm (2 in.) strip of *Velcro* or hooks and eyes instead.

To make

Join the short edges of the piece of skirt fabric leaving 15cm (6 in.) open at the top of the seam for the centre back skirt opening. Press the seam to one side. Neaten the cut ends of the ribbon. Gather the waist edge of the skirt to fit the ribbon strip. Lap one long edge of the ribbon over the gathered skirt edge and stitch in place. Sew the *Velcro* or hooks and eyes to the ends of the ribbon where they overlap.

Try the skirt on the child and turn up the hem edge if necessary so that the skirt almost touches the floor. Cut off the excess length leaving enough for a hem then hem the raw edge.

Underskirt

Make as for the skirt from old sheeting if available. Gather the waist edge and sew to a length of tape leaving enough tape at each end for tying the underskirt round the waist.

Apron

Materials required for height 147cm (4 ft 10 in.)
58cm ($\frac{5}{8}$ yd) of 92cm (36 in.) wide white cotton fabric.
2·1m ($2\frac{1}{4}$ yd) of lace edging.
1·6m ($1\frac{3}{4}$ yd) of 2·5cm (1 in.) wide ribbon or tape for the apron strings.

To make

Gather one 92cm (36 in.) edge to measure about 25cm (10 in.) for the top edge of the apron. Try the apron against the child and cut a little off the lower edge if the apron appears to be too long. Hem all the raw edges except for the gathered edge and sew on the lace edging. Lap the centre part of the length of ribbon over the gathered edge of the apron and stitch in place leaving ties at each end for tying round the waist.

Cape

Materials required for height 147cm (4 ft 10-in.)
1·4m ($1\frac{1}{2}$ yd) of 92cm (36 in.) wide red fabric.
4·6m (5 yd) of braid or bias binding for trimming the edges of the cape (this can be omitted if desired).
92cm (1 yd) of red ribbon for the cape ties.

To make

Fold the fabric in half across the width and cut the

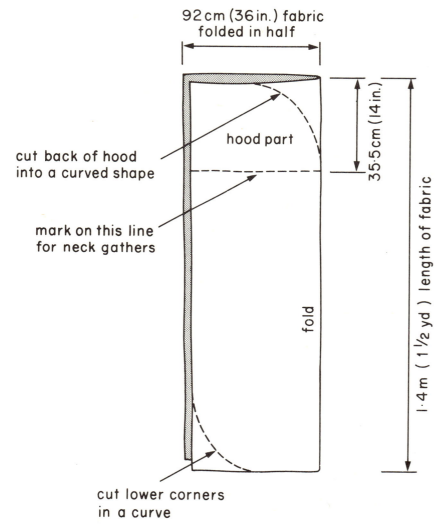

92 cm (36 in.) fabric
folded in half

hood part

35·5 cm (14 in.)

cut back of hood
into a curved shape

mark on this line
for neck gathers

fold

1·4 m (1½ yd) length of fabric

cut lower corners
in a curve

ends in to curved shapes for the hood and lower edges as shown in diagram 1. Mark a line on the fabric 35·5cm (14 in.) down from the top edge as shown in the diagram. Join the top raw edges including the curve for the back of the hood making the seam a French seam. Try the cape on the child and cut the lower edge if it is too long. Make narrow hems on all the remaining raw edges and sew on the braid.

Gather the fabric along the marked line to measure about 46cm (18 in.). Cut the ribbon in two pieces and sew one to each end of the gathers to tie the cape at the front.

Bonnet

Materials required to fit any size.
Strip of stiff interlining 18cm by 46cm (7 in. by 18 in.) for the brim shape.
46cm ($\frac{1}{2}$ yd) of 92cm (36 in.) wide black fabric.
1·4m (1$\frac{1}{2}$ yd) of lace edging about 5cm (2 in.) in width.
92cm (1 yd) of 2·5cm (1 in.) wide black ribbon for the bonnet ties.
70cm ($\frac{3}{4}$ yd) of black bias binding.
23cm ($\frac{1}{4}$ yd) of narrow elastic.
Adhesive.

To make
Make a pattern for the bonnet brim by drawing out a 33cm (13 in.) radius quarter circle with a 25·5cm (10 in.) radius quarter circle at the centre as shown in diagram 2. Round off the corners as shown in the diagram then cut the brim shape from interlining.

Spread a little adhesive all round the edge of the brim shape and stick it on to a piece of the black fabric. Cut out the fabric flush with the brim shape

all round. Cover the other side of the brim in the same way. Bind the outer edge of the brim with bias binding.

For the back of the bonnet cut a 56cm (22 in.) diameter semi-circle of black fabric. Hem the straight edge and thread the 23cm ($\frac{1}{4}$ yd) of elastic through securing the elastic at each end with a few stitches. Gather up the curved edge to fit the inner edge of the brim then sew in place. Cut the ribbon in two pieces and sew one to each side of the bonnet on the brim forming the ribbon in to a few decorative loops.

Fold the lace edging in half along the length and gather the long folded edge to fit the inner edge of the brim. Sew the lace frill in place.

Spectacles

Old fashioned metal spectacle frames are ideal if available. Alternatively a suitable pair of cheap sun glasses with the lenses removed will do.

The basket

Materials: A cardboard grocery box cut down to measure about 40cm by 28cm (16 in. by 11 in.) by 5cm (2 in.) deep.
1·4m (1$\frac{1}{2}$ yd) of 5cm (2 in.) wide hessian carpet binding to cover the outside of the cardboard.
A long boot lace for the shoulder strap.
Adhesive.

To make
Glue the boot lace underneath the box and up the short sides as shown in the illustration adjusting the length of the boot lace to suit the child. Glue the carpet

2. The brim pattern

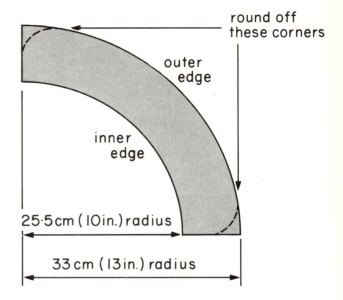

round off
these corners

outer
edge

inner
edge

25·5cm (10in.) radius

33 cm (13in.) radius

binding round the outside of the box to cover the cardboard.

The basket illustrated contains the following items. *Old things* – trinket boxes, spectacles, photo frame, beads, brooch, buckles, bracelet, cards of buttons, wooden doll, lace trimmings and braids, hair combs, shoe horn, button hook. *New things* – corset laces, lace edging, small bottles, packets of needles, tape measure, scissors, crochet hook, threads and spools of sewing cotton, wooden clothes pegs.

Hairstyle

The hair should be hidden by the bonnet.

Bathing suit,
c 1880

Bathing suits of this period were made from woollen fabrics such as flannel or serge and they must have made swimming almost impossible!

Blue cotton fabric is used for the costume illustrated, trimmed with red ric-rac braid and white tape. Navy blue is also a suitable colour.

Bathing suit top and pants

Materials required for height 147cm (4 ft 10-in.)
3·5m (3¾ yd) of 92cm (36 in.) wide cotton fabric.
6m (6½ yd) of white tape about 1·3cm (½ in.) wide.
7·3m (8 yd) of red ric-rac braid.
70cm (¾ yd) of 1·3cm (½ in.) wide elastic for the pants waist.
1·2m (1¼ yd) of narrow elastic.
Hooks and eyes for fastenings.

To make the top
Cut a 13cm (5 in.) wide strip of fabric long enough to go round the child's chest plus 8cm (3 in.). Fold the strip in half along the length bringing the long raw edges together. Join the short ends of the strip and turn right side out. Tack the long raw edges of the strip together then press it.

For the shoulder straps cut a 13cm by 61cm (5 in. by 24 in.) strip of fabric. Fold the strip in half along the length, join the long raw edges then turn right side out and press. Cut the strip in to two pieces. Put the chest band around the child's chest and overlap and pin the edges at the centre back. Pin a strap to the front and back of the chest band over each shoulder shortening the straps as necessary to make the band fit closely under the arms. Sew the ends of the straps in position on the inside of the chest band.

For the sleeves make a pattern by first drawing out a

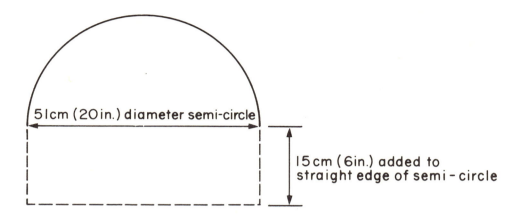

51cm (20in.) diameter semi-circle

15cm (6in.) added to
straight edge of semi-circle

51cm (20 in.) diameter semicircle. Add 15cm (6 in.) to the straight edge of the semi-circle as shown in diagram 1.

Using this pattern cut two sleeves from fabric. Turn in the lower straight edge of each sleeve 8cm (3 in.), press, then stitch the raw edge in place. Make another row of stitching on the double thickness of fabric 1·3cm ($\frac{1}{2}$ in.) away from the first row. This forms a casing for the elastic. Sew a strip of tape close to the straight edge of each sleeve. Thread a length of elastic through the casing in each sleeve to fit the child's upper arms. Secure the elastic at each end with a few stitches. Join the 8cm (3 in.) straight edges of each sleeve then turn right side out.

Gather the remaining curved raw edge of each sleeve to fit against the armhole edges of the bathing suit top

23

2. *Fitting the gathered sleeve edge to the armhole edge of the shoulder strap and chest band*

gather top curved edge of
sleeve to fit armhole edges

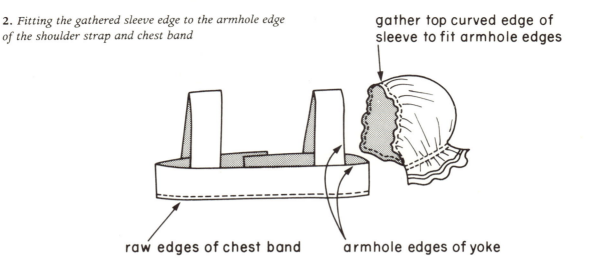

raw edges of chest band   armhole edges of yoke

as shown in diagram 2. Turn in the gathered raw edges of the sleeves and slip stitch them in place.

Stitch ric-rac braid and tape to the shoulder straps and chest band as illustrated.

For the skirt part of the bathing suit top cut two 92cm (36 in.) wide pieces of fabric by the length from the lower edge of the chest band to about 15cm (6 in.) above the child's knees. Join the skirt pieces together at the short edges then cut one piece in half as shown in diagram 3. Join these edges again to within 10cm (4 in.) of the top edges, thus forming the back opening. Press the seam to one side.

Gather the top edge of the skirt to fit the lower edge of the chest band and sew it in place. Hem the lower edge and sew on tape and ric-rac braid. Sew hooks and eyes to the back overlap of the chest band.

24

To make the pants

Measurements for the pants pattern shown in diagram 4 are given in three sizes. The smallest size is first and the medium and large sizes follow in brackets. Draw out the pattern to the size required noting that it does not matter if the pants are a little too big since the fullness is taken up with elastic at the waist and knee edges. Try the pattern against the child for leg length and shorten if necessary but note that 8cm (3 in.) extra should be left on the length to allow for the turning.

Cut two pants pieces from fabric placing the long edge of the pattern against a fold in the fabric each time. Turn in the lower edge of each piece 8cm (3 in.), press, stitch, sew on tape and thread through elastic in the same way as for the sleeves.

Join the pants pieces to each other at the centre edges then bring these seams together and join the inside leg edges. Turn in and hem the waist edge to form a casing for the 1·3cm (½ in.) wide elastic. Thread the elastic through to fit the child's waist.

3. *Joining the skirt pieces together and cutting one piece in half*

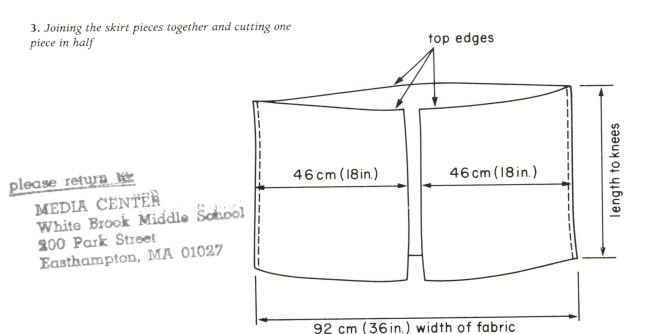

top edges

46 cm (18 in.)   46 cm (18 in.)

length to knees

92 cm (36 in.) width of fabric

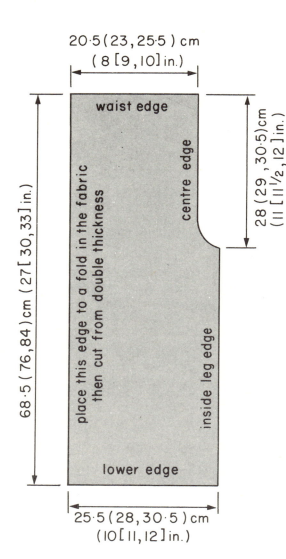

20·5 (23 , 25·5) cm
(8 [9 , 10] in.)

waist edge

centre edge

place this edge to a fold in the fabric then cut from double thickness

68·5 (76 , 84) cm (27 [30 , 33] in.)

28 (29 , 30·5) cm (11 [11½ , 12] in.)

inside leg edge

lower edge

25·5 (28 , 30·5) cm
(10 [11 , 12] in.)

4. *The pants pattern*

Bathing cap

Materials required to fit any size.
A 46cm (18 in.) diameter circle of fabric.
46cm ($\frac{1}{2}$ yd) of narrow elastic.
1·6cm (1$\frac{3}{4}$ yd) of narrow lace edging.

To make

Turn in the raw edge of the fabric circle 1·3cm ($\frac{1}{2}$ in.) and stitch forming a casing for the elastic. Sew the lace trimming to the folded edge of the circle. Thread through the elastic to fit the child's head.

Bathing shoes

Use a pair of cheap plastic slippers sewing on tapes or ribbons to lace up the legs as shown in the illustration.

Spanish
costume

A plain red sleeveless T-shirt with a low neckline is the basis for the bodice of this dress but one with short sleeves would also be suitable. Matching cotton seersucker fabric is used for the skirt and the sleeve frills. Red striped or checked fabric could be used instead.

Dress

Materials required for height 147cm (4 ft 10 in.).
5·5m (6 yd) of 92cm (36 in.) wide cotton fabric.
A plain T-shirt which matches the cotton fabric.
14m (15 yd) of white trimming, this can be lace edging, ric-rac braid or white tape etc.
2 hooks and eyes.
15cm (6 in.) of *Velcro*.

To make the skirt

For the basic skirt cut two 35·5cm by 92cm (14 in. by 36 in.) strips of fabric. Note that for smaller sizes the 35·5cm (14 in.) measurement should be the child's measurement from the hip to above the knee. Join the short edges of the strips leaving a 10cm (4-in.) gap at the top of one seam for the centre back opening of the skirt. Gather the upper edge to fit the child's hip measurement plus 2·5cm (1 in.).

For the hem frill cut four 40·5cm by 92cm (16 in. by 36 in.) strips of fabric. Note that for smaller sizes the 40·5cm (16 in.) measurement should be the measurement from the lower edge of the basic skirt to just above the ankles. Join the strips together at the short edges forming a continuous piece. Hem one long raw edge and sew on the white trimming. Gather the remaining long raw edge to fit the lower edge of the skirt and sew it in place.

For the top frill cut three 25·5cm by 92cm (10 in. by

36 in.) strips of fabric. Make this frill a little narrower for smaller sizes. Make up and trim the frill in the same way as given for the hem frill. Gather the remaining long raw edge to fit the top gathered edge of the skirt and sew it in place having the raw edges even.

Cut out and make the middle frill in the same way as given for the hem frill. Gather the remaining long raw edge to fit the basic skirt and pin it in place about half way up the skirt positioning it so that the hem frill will be the widest, the middle frill a little narrower and the top frill the narrowest. Sew the gathered edge of the middle frill in place.

Bind the top raw edges of the skirt with a strip of lace edging or a strip of the cotton fabric. Sew hooks and eyes to the back overlap.

Cut the hooked side of the *Velcro* strip in to 2·5cm (1 in.) pieces and sew them inside the top edge of the skirt having one at each side, two evenly spaced at the front and two at the back. This is for fixing the skirt to the T-shirt when the dress is worn.

To make the bodice

Gather a 92cm (1 yd) length of lace edging to fit the neck edge of the T-shirt and sew it in place. Alternatively, a narrow strip of cotton fabric may be used instead of lace edging.

For each sleeve cut a 10cm by 51cm (4 in. by 20 in.) strip of cotton fabric. Join the 10cm (4 in.) edges of each strip. Gather one long edge to fit the armhole or sleeve edge of the T-shirt and sew it in place.

For each sleeve frill cut a 20·5cm by 92cm (8 in. by 36 in.) strip of cotton fabric. Join the 20·5cm (8 in.) edges of each strip. Hem one long edge and sew on trimming. Gather the remaining raw edge to fit the sleeve and sew it in place.

1. Glueing a piece of card to the comb to give it height

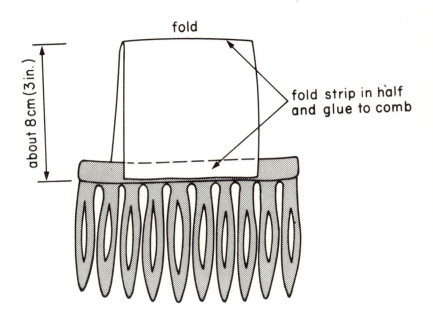

fold

fold strip in half
and glue to comb

about 8cm (3 in.)

Put the bodice on the child then put on the skirt. Mark the position of the *Velcro* strips on the T-shirt. Sew 2·5cm (1 in.) pieces of the furry strip of Velcro to the T-shirt at the marked positions.

Socks and shoes

White socks and plain black shoes can be worn.

Hair and mantilla

The hair should be secured in a bun at the crown of the head. A comb is then fixed in to the bun. An ordinary side comb can be used for this but to give it extra height glue on a strip of strong card folded in half as shown in diagram 1.

The lace mantilla may be black or white and either dress fabric or curtain lace is suitable. Fold in half, corner to corner, a 92cm (36 in.) square of lace fabric to make a triangle. Note that if the fabric used is heavy it may be best to cut the lace fabric in half as folded and use only one triangular piece.

Drape the triangle of fabric over the comb having the longest edge of the triangle at the front edge of the hair. Catch the mantilla to the top edge of the comb with a few small stitches.

Accessories

Castanets, a tambourine or a fan can be carried.

Puritan costume, c 1655

A plain grey school sweater is used for the top of the dress and the skirt is made from matching grey fabric. Brown is also a suitable colour. The white apron, collar, cuffs and cap are all made from an old cotton sheet but yardage is given in the materials required lists in case the fabric has to be bought. The high crowned hat, worn by both men and women of the time, is made from stiff interlining covered with black brushed nylon.

Dress top

Use a grey or brown long sleeved sweater.

Dress skirt

Materials required for height 147cm (4 ft 10 in.).
1·9m (2 yd) of 92cm (36 in.) wide fabric the same colour as the sweater.
A length of 2·5cm (1 in.) wide petersham ribbon to match the fabric, the child's waist measurement plus 5cm (2 in.) for an overlap.
5cm (2 in.) strip of *Velcro* or hooks and eyes instead.

To make

Join the short edges of the piece of skirt fabric leaving 15cm (6 in.) open at the top of the seam for the centre back skirt opening. Press the seam to one side. Neaten the cut ends of the ribbon. Gather the waist edge of the skirt to fit the ribbon strip. Lap one long edge of the ribbon over the gathered skirt edge and stitch in place. Sew the *Velcro* or hooks and eyes to the ends of the ribbon where they overlap.

 Try the skirt on the child and turn up the hem edge if necessary so that the skirt almost touches the floor.

1. The cap

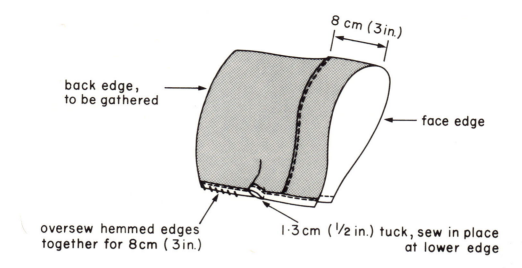

back edge, to be gathered

8 cm (3 in.)

face edge

oversew hemmed edges together for 8cm (3 in.)

1·3 cm (½ in.) tuck, sew in place at lower edge

Cut off the excess length leaving enough for a hem then hem the raw edge.

Underskirt

Make as for the skirt from old sheeting if available. Gather the waist edge and sew to a length of tape leaving enough tape at each end for tying the skirt round the waist.

Cap

A 38cm by 51cm (15 in. by 20 in.) strip of white cotton fabric is required for the cap which will fit any size. Turn in one 51cm (20 in.) edge 8cm (3 in.) and press. Turn in the raw edge and stitch in place. Make a narrow hem along each of the 38cm (15 in.) raw edges. Fold the strip of fabric in half bringing the hemmed edges together and oversew the edges together for 8cm (3 in.) as shown in diagram 1.

Make a 1·3cm (½ in.) tuck in the hemmed edges at each side as shown in diagram 1 and oversew the tucks in place at the lower edge.

Turn the cap inside out and run a gathering thread round the back edge. Pull up the gathers tightly and fasten off the thread. Turn the cap right side out. Turn back the face edge about 5cm (2 in.) when the cap is worn.

33

2. The collar pattern

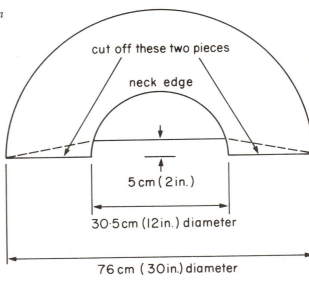

cut off these two pieces

neck edge

5 cm (2 in.)

30·5 cm (12 in.) diameter

76 cm (30 in.) diameter

Collar

Materials required for height 147cm (4 ft 10 in.).
92cm (1 yd) of 92cm (36 in.) wide white cotton
fabric.
1·9m (2 yd) of lace edging.
2·5cm (1 in.) strip of *Velcro* or hooks and eyes
instead.

To make
Make a pattern for the collar by drawing out a 76cm
(30 in.) diameter semicircle with a 30·5cm (12 in.)
diameter semicircle at the centre. Cut a piece off
each of the straight edges of the pattern as shown in
diagram 2. Try this pattern on the child and trim off

3. *Cutting the cuff pieces*

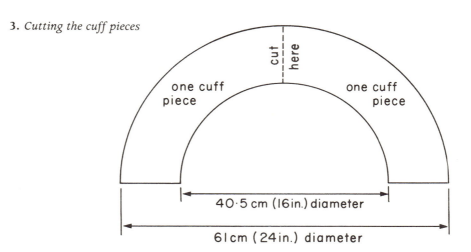

one cuff piece   cut here   one cuff piece

40·5 cm (16 in.) diameter

61 cm (24 in.) diameter

the outer edge as necessary if the collar appears to be too large.

Cut the collar from double fabric. Join the collar pieces together round all the edges leaving a gap in the seam for turning. Trim the seams and clip the curves. Turn the collar right side out and turn in the remaining raw edges and slip stitch.

Press the collar then sew lace trimming to all the edges except for the neck edge. Sew the strip of *Velcro* or hooks and eyes to the front neck edge.

Turn in the back neck edge of the collar when it is worn.

Cuffs

Materials required to fit any size.
35cm ($\frac{3}{8}$ yd) of 92cm (36 in.) wide white cotton fabric.
5cm (2 in.) strip of *Velcro* or hooks and eyes instead.

To make

Make a pattern for the cuffs by drawing out a 61cm (24 in.) diameter semicircle with a 40·5cm (16 in.) diameter semicircle at the centre. Cut this pattern piece from fabric, then cut the fabric piece in half as shown in diagram 3 to make two cuff pieces.

Fold each cuff piece in half bringing the straight edges together. Join the raw edges leaving a gap in the seam for turning. Trim the seams and clip the curves then turn the cuffs right side out. Turn in the remaining raw edges and slip stitch.

Press the cuffs then oversew the straight edges of each cuff together to within 4cm ($1\frac{1}{2}$ in.) of the wrist edges. Sew *Velcro* or hooks and eyes to these openings.

Apron

Materials required for height 147cm (4 ft 10 in.).
70cm (¾ yd) of 92cm (36 in.) wide white cotton fabric.
1·4m (1½ yd) of white bias binding.

To make

The 92cm (36 in.) width of the fabric is the length of the apron. For smaller sizes cut the apron length to come about 5cm (2 in.) above the skirt hem leaving enough fabric to make a deep hem on the lower edge of the apron.

Hem the lower edge then make narrow turnings on the sides of the apron. Gather the upper edge to measure about 20·5cm (8 in.). Bind the gathered top edge with the bias binding at the centre of the length of binding. Fold the remainder of the binding at each end in half and stitch, forming the apron ties.

Hat

Materials required to fit any size.
46cm (½ yd) of 82cm (32 in.) wide stiff interlining.
A 35·5cm (14 in.) square of thin card.
70cm (¾ yd) of 92cm (36 in.) wide black brushed nylon or other black fabric for covering the hat.
Strip of grey ribbon, bias strip of fabric or bias binding for the hat band.
1·9m (2 yd) of black bias binding.

To make

Make a pattern for the tapered crown of the hat by drawing out a 40·5cm (16 in.) radius quarter circle with a 25·5cm (10 in.) radius quarter circle at the centre as shown in diagram 4. Cut this shape from

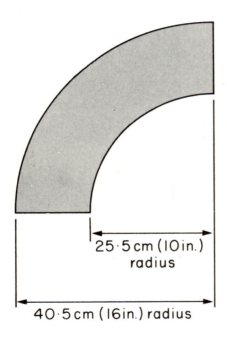

25·5cm (10in.)
radius

40·5cm (16in.) radius

4. *The hat crown pattern*

interlining. Bring the straight edges together and over-lap them slightly forming the tapered shape.

Place the white cap on the child's head and on top of this place the tapered hat shape in the correct position as shown in the illustration. Lap the straight edges of the crown as necessary to make it fit the head. Cut the excess interlining off at one straight edge leaving only 1·3cm ($\frac{1}{2}$ in.) extra for an overlap. To cover the crown piece spread a little adhesive all round the edges and stick it on to a piece of the hat fabric. Cut out the fabric allowing 0·6cm ($\frac{1}{4}$ in.) extra fabric all round the interlining shape. Turn this extra 0·6cm ($\frac{1}{4}$ in.) over and stick it on to the other side of the interlining. Overlap the straight edges of the crown piece 1·3cm ($\frac{1}{2}$ in.) and sew in place.

For the top of the hat cut a circle of interlining to fit the top of the crown piece. Cover the circle with fabric in the same way as given for the crown piece. Oversew the edge of the circle in position on top of the crown piece.

For the brim of the hat cut a 35·5cm (14 in.) dia-meter circle of interlining then cut a 16·5cm ($6\frac{1}{2}$ in.) diameter circle from the centre and discard it. Glue this brim shape on to the piece of thin card and cut out the card even with the shape. Place the hat crown in position on the brim and if necessary make the 16·5cm ($6\frac{1}{2}$ in.) diameter hole in the brim larger to fit the lower edge of the hat crown. Note that the hat will fit better if the hole is enlarged in to an oval shape as shown in diagram 5.

Spread a little adhesive round the outer and inner edges of the brim shape then stick it on to a piece of the hat fabric. Cut out the fabric even with the inter-lining shape. Cover the other side of the brim in the same way. Bind the outer edge of the brim with bias binding.

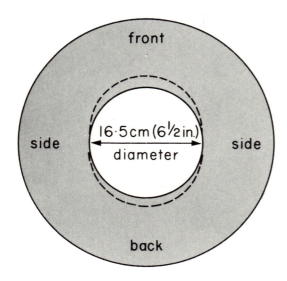

5. *Enlarging the hole in the hat brim to make it oval shaped*

Oversew the lower edge of the crown to the inner edge of the brim. Glue a strip of bias binding over this join, on the inside of the hat to neaten it.

Sew the grey hat band in position on the outside of the hat.

Hairstyle

The hair should be hidden beneath the cap.

Ancient Egyptian costume

White butter muslin is used double for the dress and cape illustrated, but any kind of fine cotton fabric in pastel colours would be suitable. The collar and bracelets are made by sticking a variety of gold, red and blue braids and cords on to stiff interlining shapes. Ring-pulls, saved from the tops of drinks cans and painted gold, also make a very effective decoration on the collar. Alternatively beads, buttons, curtain rings, paper clips etc., can be used.

If the child has naturally dark hair the wig can be omitted and only the head band needs to be made.

Dress and shoulder cape

Materials required for height 147cm (4 ft 10 in.).
5·8m (6¼ yd) of 92cm (36 in.) wide butter muslin; note that only half this yardage is required if thicker cotton fabric is used.
70cm (¾ yd) of narrow elastic.
One hook and eye.
70cm (¾ yd) of narrow tape for the dress shoulder straps.

To make the dress

Cut two pieces of muslin 92cm (36 in.) wide by twice the child's underarm to ankle measurement. Join these two pieces at the long edges forming a long tube of fabric. Hem the remaining raw edges at each end of the tube. Fold the tube in half back on itself to form a double thickness tube having the right side of the fabric outside. Hem the top folded edge of the tube to form a casing for the elastic then thread elastic through to fit the child's chest.

Put the dress on the child and attach lengths of tape to the top of the dress to go over each shoulder to hold the dress up.

1. The cape pattern

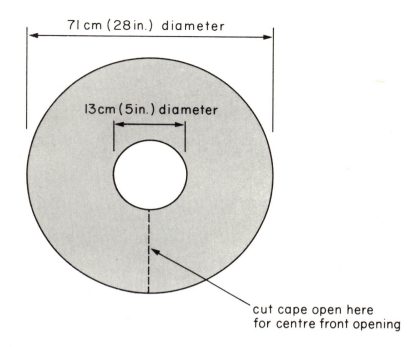

71 cm (28 in.) diameter

13 cm (5 in.) diameter

cut cape open here
for centre front opening

To make the cape

Make a pattern for the cape by drawing out a 71cm
(28 in.) diameter circle with a 13cm (5 in.) diameter
circle cut out of the centre. Cut the cape from double
thickness muslin then make a cut from the outer to
the inner edge as shown in diagram 1.

Join the two cape pieces round the inner and outer
curved edges leaving the straight front edges open.
Turn right side out and press. Turn in the front edges
and run a gathering thread along each one, pull up
the gathers tightly and fasten off the threads. Sew a
hook and eye to the gathered edges.

41

2. *The collar pattern*

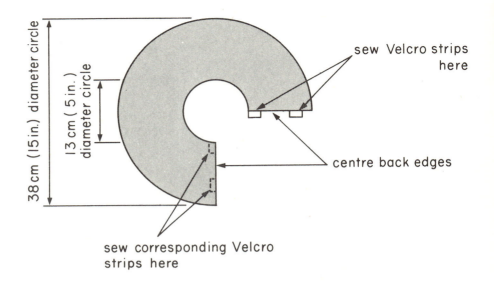

38cm (15 in.) diameter circle

13 cm (5 in.) diameter circle

sew Velcro strips here

centre back edges

sew corresponding Velcro strips here

Girdle

For this use 2 to 3m (yd) of silky gold coloured cord. Knot and fringe out the ends of the cord then tie the girdle round the waist as illustrated.

Collar

Materials required to fit any size.
46cm ($\frac{1}{2}$ yd) of 82cm (32 in.) wide stiff interlining.
Oddment of gold coloured fabric at least 40·5cm (16 in.) square for covering the collar shape.
5cm (2 in.) strip of *Velcro*.
Ric-rac braids, cords, tapes, coloured paper or cord or any suitable materials for trimming the collar.
Adhesive.

To make

Cut a 38cm (15 in.) diameter circle of interlining then cut a 13cm (5 in.) diameter circle from the centre and discard it. Cut away one quarter of the remaining shape to give the collar shape shown in diagram 2.

Spread adhesive all round the edges of the shape and stick it on the piece of gold fabric. Cut out the fabric allowing 1·3cm ($\frac{1}{2}$ in.) extra all round the collar shape. Turn the 1·3cm ($\frac{1}{2}$ in.) extra on to the other side of the collar and stick it in place. Sew on two 2·5cm (1 in.) strips of *Velcro* at the positions indicated in diagram 2.

Now glue trimmings etc. to the collar. The ring-pulls in the collar illustrated have circles of red paper glued in the rings and, in between them, triangles of blue paper. Metal pieces may require a preliminary coat of glue which should be left to dry before finally sticking the pieces to the collar.

Bracelets

Materials required to fit any size.
Small pieces of stiff interlining and gold coloured fabric.
Two 5cm (2 in.) strips of *Velcro*.
Braids and cords as for the collar.
Adhesive.

To make
Cut two 6·5cm (2½ in.) wide strips of interlining by the child's wrist measurement plus 1·3cm (½ in.). Cover the pieces with fabric and glue on trimmings in the same way as given for the collar. Sew a strip of *Velcro* to each bracelet at the short edges.

Sandals

The feet can be bare but sandals are easy to make using as a basis plastic flip-flop sandals.

First remove the plastic toe straps on the sandals and replace these with strips of narrow braid going from the toe hole to the arch of the foot. Another strip of braid goes across the foot and then the first strip is joined on to it as shown in diagram 3. Knot the ends of the braid tightly underneath the soles, the

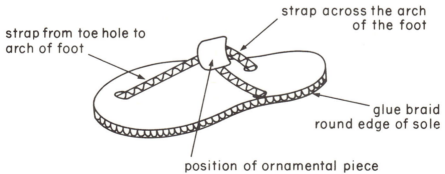

strap across the arch
of the foot

strap from toe hole to
arch of foot

glue braid
round edge of sole

position of ornamental piece

3. *Making the sandals*

43

4. *Winding the wool round the piece of card*

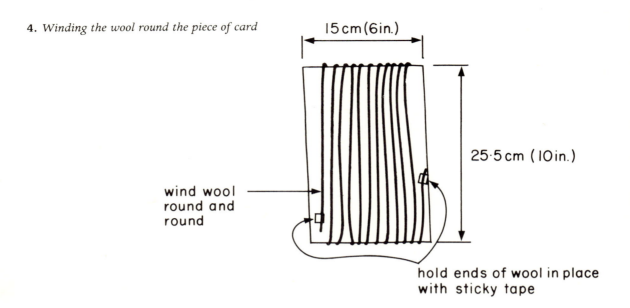

15 cm (6 in.)

25·5 cm (10 in.)

wind wool round and round

hold ends of wool in place with sticky tape

knots will sink in to the recesses there. Glue strips of braid round the edges of the soles. Make a small ornamental piece for each sandal in the same way as for the collar using small strips of interlining as foundations. Glue the ornamental pieces in place on the straps as shown in diagram 3.

The wig

Materials required to fit any size.
Two 50 gramme balls of black double, double knitting wool or yarn.
A circle of black fabric about 30·5cm (12 in.) in diameter.
A 2·5cm (1 in.) wide strip of stiff interlining long enough to go round the child's head plus 2·5cm (1 in.), for the headband.
Gold fabric for covering the headband.
1·4m (1½ yd) of gold ric-rac braid.
Adhesive.

To make

For the headband cover the strip of interlining with fabric in the same way as given for the collar.

For the lengths of hair which hang down all round, make a template of cardboard measuring 25·5cm by 15cm (10 in. by 6 in.). Cut a 3m (3 yd) length of wool and wind it round and round the card as shown in diagram 4, holding the ends in place with bits of sticky tape. Now *very carefully* steam this wool using

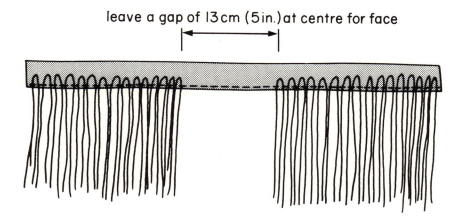

leave a gap of 13cm (5in.) at centre for face

either a steam iron or steam from a kettle spout. This will make the wool strands quite straight but take care not to get burned.

Cut through the wool strands at one end of the card and carefully take the folded ends and stitch them to the inside of the headband as shown in diagram 5. Continue making wool strands and sewing them to the head band in this way until it is completed, leaving a gap of about 13cm (5 in.) at the centre of the band for the face.

Now place the band around the child's head, overlap the back edges as necessary to fit then stitch them together. Glue two rows of gold ric-rac to the band.

For the top part of the wig, place the 30·5cm (12 in.) diameter circle of black fabric on top of the child's head and then put the headband in position over it. Mark the position of the top edge of the headband on to the fabric circle all round. Remove the fabric and cut it out 1·3cm (½ in.) larger all round than the marked shape. The final shape will be slightly oval.

To cover this oval shape with wool, wind strands of the remaining wool around the card, steam, then cut through the wool strands at both ends. Stitch the wool strands to the centre of the oval of fabric as shown in diagram 6. Continue until the fabric is completely

6. *Stitching the wool strands to the oval of fabric*

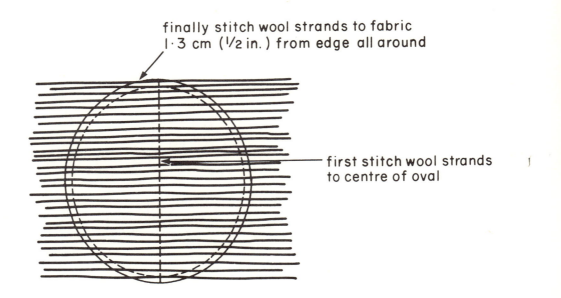

finally stitch wool strands to fabric
1·3 cm (½ in.) from edge all around

first stitch wool strands
to centre of oval

7. *Sewing the top of the wig to the headband*

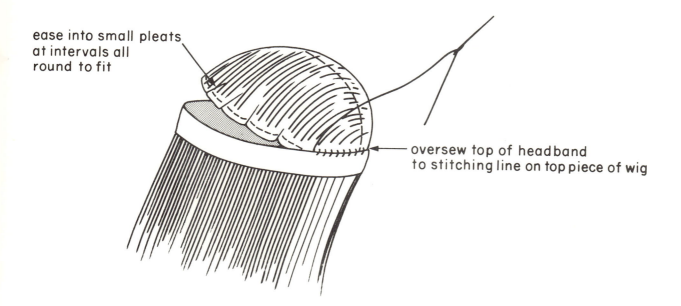

ease into small pleats
at intervals all
round to fit

oversew top of headband
to stitching line on top piece of wig

covered. Now stitch the wool strands to the fabric all round 1·3cm ($\frac{1}{2}$ in.) from the edge as shown in diagram 6. Cut the wool strands level with the fabric shape all round.

Lap the top of the headband 1·3cm ($\frac{1}{2}$ in.) over the raw edge of the oval shape and slip stitch it in place as shown in diagram 7 easing the fabric in to small pleats as intervals to make it fit. Note that the stitch-

47

ing for the centre 'parting' of the wig should be in line with the centre front of the headband.

Finally, once more steam the lengths of wool and cut the ends to an even length all round.

If the child has long hair, gather it to the nape of the neck and pin in a flat bun so that it is hidden by the wig.

Make-up

Use face cream and talcum powder to whiten the face then colour the cheeks and mouth with orange lipstick. Colour the area above the eyes with green eye shadow then outline the eyes and eyebrows with black, extending the lines outward at the outer corners of the eyes.

Japanese
costume

The kimono can be made from plain or patterned fabric and in any colour. The obi or sash should be in a bright contrasting colour. Curtain brocade in soft pink and fawn is used for the kimono illustrated here, with an orange satin obi. The whole outfit is very quick and easy to make.

Kimono and obi

Materials required for height 147cm (4 ft 10-in.). 3m (3¼ yd) of 122cm (48 in.) wide fabric. Note that for a smaller child 92cm (36 in.) wide fabric may be wide enough – see the diagrams for measurements. 92cm (1 yd) of 92cm (36 in.) or 122cm (48 in.) wide fabric for the obi.

1. *Folding the fabric and cutting out the neck shape*

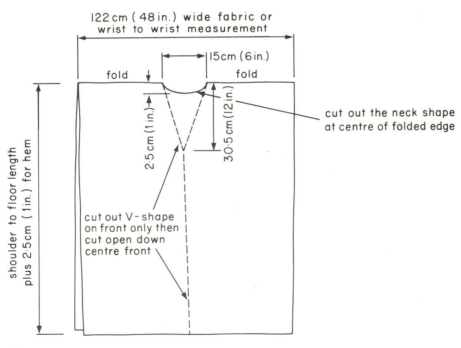

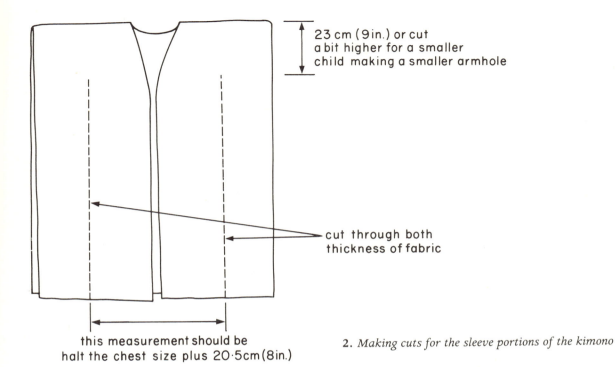

23 cm (9 in.) or cut
a bit higher for a smaller
child making a smaller armhole

cut through both
thickness of fabric

this measurement should be
halt the chest size plus 20·5cm (8 in.)

2. *Making cuts for the sleeve portions of the kimono*

To make the kimono

Fold the fabric in half bringing the 122cm (48 in.) edges together and having the wrong side outside. Cut out the curved neck shape as shown by the solid line in diagram 1. Next cut out the V-neck shape on the front only then cut open down the centre front as shown by the dotted lines in diagram 1.

Make cuts for the sleeve portions of the kimono from the hem edge upwards as shown by the dotted lines in diagram 2. Trim the length of the sleeves so that they will be about knee length when the kimono is worn as shown in diagram 3. Keep these remnants of fabric for use later on.

Join the kimono seams as shown in diagram 4 leaving 18cm (7 in.) open at the wrist edges. Clip the seams at the corners then turn the kimono and sleeves right side out and press. Turn in and hem the wrist edges, the hem edge and the centre front edges up to the beginning of the V-neckline.

From the remnants of fabric left over from the sleeves, cut 15cm (6 in.) wide strips, joining them as

51

3. *Cutting the sleeves to make them knee length*

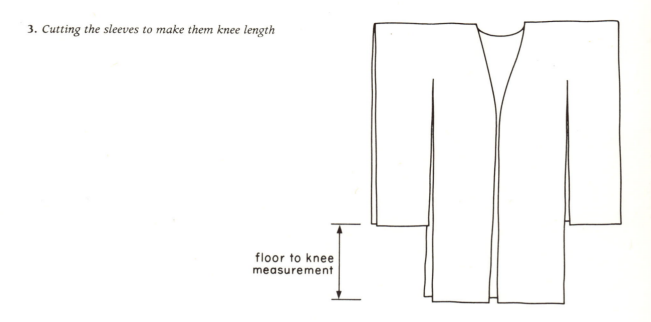

floor to knee
measurement

necessary to make a band long enough to fit round the neck and down the V-shaped front edges. Fold the strip in half bringing the long edges together then stitch across the short ends. Turn the strip right side out and press. Sew the long edges of the band in position all round the neck of the kimono having the right sides together and raw edges even. Press the seam downwards and the band up.

When worn, the left front of the kimono should be wrapped right over the right front and held in place with the obi. To make walking easier an extra length of fabric made up from remnants may be added to the right front of the kimono as shown in diagram 5.

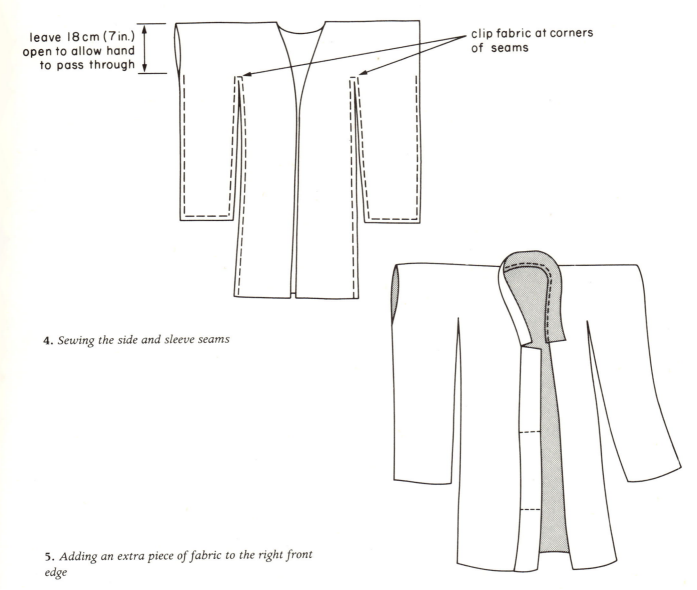

leave 18 cm (7 in.) open to allow hand to pass through

clip fabric at corners of seams

4. *Sewing the side and sleeve seams*

5. *Adding an extra piece of fabric to the right front edge*

53

To make the obi

Cut the fabric in to three 30·5cm (12 in.) by 92cm (36 in.) or 122cm (48 in.) strips according to the width of fabric used. Join the strips at the short edges to make a continuous strip. Turn in and hem all the raw edges.

Lay the strip flat, fold the long edges in toward each other and press, having the right side of the fabric outside.

Wind the folded obi three times round the body as shown in the illustration then tie the two ends once at the back. Push the remaining ends up through the obi making large loops of fabric. Alternatively, the ends may be tied in a butterfly bow. A fan may be tucked inside the top edge of the obi.

Sandals

Flip-flop sandals are most suitable.

Hair and Make-up

Dress the hair as shown in the illustration sweeping it in to loops at the front and sides. Pin real or artificial flowers and grasses in the hair. Use black eyeliner on the eyelids to give a slant-eyed look and colour the mouth with lipstick at the centre part only.

1920s
evening dress

This outfit is quick and easy to make using satin dress lining fabric for the basic dress and curtain net in the same colour for the 'handkerchief panels' skirt. The dress illustrated is in vivid orange but any bright colour is suitable. Sequin and bead trimmings were very popular at this period and these can be applied as lavishly as desired.

Dress and headband

Materials required for height 147cm (4 ft 10 in.).
1·4m (1½ yd) of 92cm (36 in.) wide satin dress lining fabric.
2·8m (3 yd) of 122cm (48 in.) wide curtain net in the same colour as the satin fabric.
2·1m (2¼ yd) of silver sequins.
2·1m (2¼ yd) of contrasting coloured sequins.
Snap fasteners for the dress back fastening and the headband.
Feather for trimming the headband if available.

To make the dress

For the dress bodice cut a rectangle of satin fabric to the measurements shown in diagram 1. Fold this bodice piece in half with the right side of the fabric outside, along the line indicated and press. The folded edge is the top edge of the bodice. Turn in the centre back raw edges 2·5cm (1 in.) and stitch in place. Sew a row of each colour of sequins round the top of the bodice as shown in the illustration.

For the bodice straps cut a 6·5cm (2½ in.) wide strip of satin fabric 61cm (24 in.) in length. Turn in each of the long raw edges of the strip 2cm (¾ in.) and press, making a 2·5cm (1 in.) wide strip. Stitch down the centre of the strip to hold the raw edges in place. Cut the strip in two pieces. Place the dress bodice

around the child and overlap and pin the back edges as necessary to make it fit. Pin the straps in position on the front and back of the bodice shortening them as necessary to make the bodice fit neatly underneath the arms. Mark the position of the ends of the straps on the bodice with pins. Sew two rows of sequins to each strap then sew the ends of the straps in position on the inside of the bodice.

For the dress skirt cut a 92cm (36 in.) wide strip of satin fabric long enough to reach from the lower edge of the dress bodice to above the child's knees. Note that for a very small child the 92cm (36 in.) width may give too much fullness in the skirt, so instead, make the skirt the child's hip measurement plus 15cm (6 in.). Join the short edges of the skirt strip leaving about 10cm (4 in.) open at the top of the seam for the back skirt opening. Press the seam to one side. Slightly gather the upper edge of the skirt until it fits the lower edge of the bodice then sew the skirt in position. Hem the lower edge of the skirt.

For the handkerchief panels on the skirt about thirty-four squares of curtain net are required. For height about 147cm (4 ft 10-in.) 30·5cm (12 in.) squares are the correct size. For much smaller sizes, cut a sample square of fabric and pin one corner of the square to the lower edge of the dress bodice. The opposite corner of the square should hang down about 10cm (4 in.) below the hem edge of the dress; if it is longer, cut the square accordingly to obtain the correct size.

Cut out the thirty-four squares of curtain net. Pin half of them in place as shown in diagram 2, spacing them out evenly all round the lower edge of the bodice. Stitch the corners of the squares in place as pinned. Now pin the remaining squares between the first lot turning in the corner of each one as

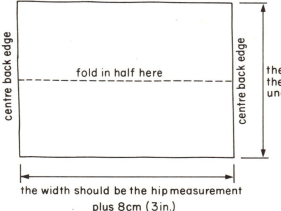

centre back edge

fold in half here

centre back edge

the length should be twice
the measurement from just
underneath the arms to the hips

the width should be the hip measurement
plus 8cm (3in.)

1. *How to cut the dress bodice piece*

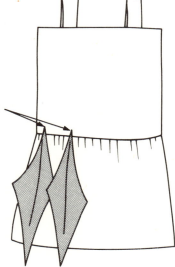

pin corners here
spacing them out evenly
all round lower edge
of bodice

necessary in order to fill in the gaps, as shown in diagram 3. Stitch the squares in position.

For the band around the hips cut a 10cm (4 in.) wide strip of net fabric long enough to go around the lower edge of the dress bodice. Join the long edges taking a 0·6cm ($\frac{1}{4}$ in.) seam. Turn the strip right side out and press. Sew one long edge of the strip in position at the lower edge of the bodice covering the top points of the handkerchief squares. Sew the short edges of the strip to the centre back edges of the bodice.

Make a bow from a scrap of the net fabric and sew

2. *Pinning the first lot of handkerchief panels in place*

57

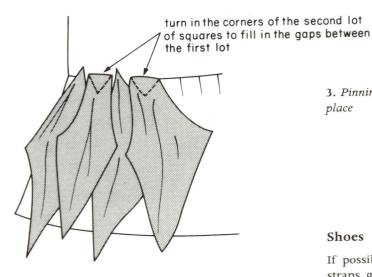

turn in the corners of the second lot of squares to fill in the gaps between the first lot

3. Pinning the second lot of handkerchief panels in place

it to the band at one side of the dress. Sew snap fasteners to the centre back overlap.

To make the headband

Using satin lining fabric make a strip in the same way as given for the bodice straps. Cut the strip to fit around the child's head leaving 4cm (1½ in.) extra for neatening the ends and an overlap. Neaten the ends then sew two rows of sequins to the strip as shown in the illustration. Sew snap fasteners to the overlap.

Make a small bow from a scrap of net fabric and sew it to one side of the headband along with the feather.

Shoes

If possible the shoes should have little heels and straps going across the instep. Alternatively plain flat slippers can be used with a band of ribbon sewn across the instep.

Jewellery

Long strings of beads, especially pearls, dangling ear-rings, and slave bangles are all suitable.

Hairstyle

Short hair is the correct style for this period but long hair can be swept up at the back and pinned as flat as possible. The headband will help to hold it in place.

Make-up

Colour the cheeks and lips with red lipstick. Eyebrows can also be pencilled in making a thin line.

Tudor
costume,
c 1530

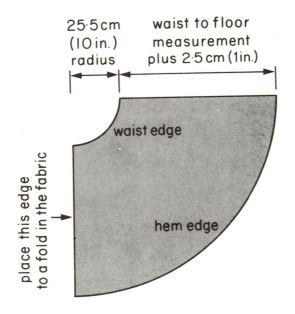

25·5cm (10 in.) radius

waist to floor measurement plus 2·5 cm (1in.)

place this edge to a fold in the fabric

waist edge

hem edge

1. *The skirt pattern*

This type of costume with the gable head-dress and huge cuffs was worn during the reign of Henry VIII. Green velvet curtain fabric is used for the dress illustrated here but plain non-woven curtain fabric would also be suitable. Other colours fashionable at the time were shades of red, orange, blue and grey. Reference can be made to costume books for more ideas about colours and fabrics. If desired, plain brocade material can be used for the turned back cuffs instead of fur fabric.

Dress

Materials required for height 147cm (4 ft 10-in.). 3m (3¼ yd) of 122cm (48 in.) wide velvet or other plain curtain fabric.

46cm (½ yd) of 122cm (48 in.) wide patterned brocade curtain fabric for the under sleeves.

92cm (1 yd) of 122cm (48 in.) wide fur fabric or brocade curtain fabric for the turned back sleeve cuffs.

Strip of cotton fabric for lining the bodice the same size as given for the bodice in the making up instructions.

2·3m (2½ yd) of 2·5cm (1 in.) wide lace edging for trimming the under sleeves and the bodice neckline.

1·4m (1½ yd) each of 2cm (¾ in.) wide braid and very narrow braid for trimming the bodice neckline. Hooks and eyes for the back bodice fastening.

46cm (½ yd) narrow elastic.

To make the skirt

Make a quarter circle paper pattern for the skirt drawing it to the sizes given in diagram 1. Place the edge of the pattern marked 'fold' against a fold in the

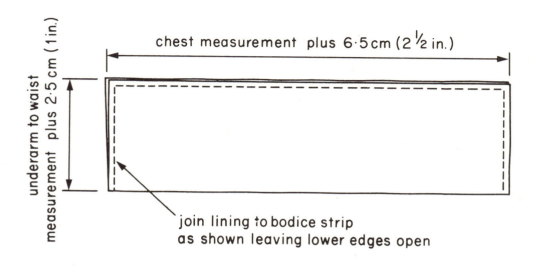

chest measurement plus 6·5 cm (2 ½ in.)

underarm to waist measurement plus 2·5 cm (1 in.)

join lining to bodice strip
as shown leaving lower edges open

2. *The bodice pattern*

velvet fabric then cut out the skirt from the double thickness of fabric to give the full size semicircular shaped skirt.

Join the straight edges of the semicircle taking a 2·5cm (1 in.) seam and leaving 15cm (6 in.) open at the waist edge of the seam for the centre back skirt opening. Press the seam to one side. Do not hem the lower edge of the skirt at this stage.

To make the bodice

Cut a strip of velvet fabric to the measurements given in diagram 2. Cut a strip of lining fabric the same size. Join the lining to the bodice strip as shown in diagram 2 leaving the waist edges open. Turn the bodice right side out and press. Tack the waist edges together.

For the shoulder straps cut a 5cm by 61cm (2 in. by 24 in.) strip of velvet fabric. Join the long raw edges of the strip, turn it right side out and press. Cut the strip in to two pieces.

Place the bodice inside out around the child's chest overlapping and pinning the short edges at the

3. *Pinning on the shoulder straps and side darts*

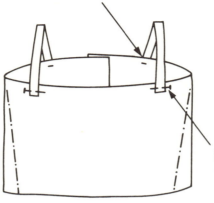

pin back edges of straps about 9 cm (3 ½ in.) in from the sides

pin front edges of straps about 8 cm (3 in.) in from the sides

centre back to fit. Pin the ends of the shoulder straps to the bodice as shown in diagram 3 shortening the straps as necessary to make the bodice fit neatly under the arms. Pin a dart in each side of the bodice through both thicknesses of fabric from the waist edge tapering to the top edge as shown in diagram 3, to make the bodice fit neatly round the waist.

Take off the bodice, stitch the darts as pinned then sew the ends of the straps in place. Sew one edge of the lace edging to the inside of the neck edge and straps as shown in the illustration.

For the sleeves make a pattern as shown in diagram 4. First of all draw out a 20·5 cm (8 in.) diameter semicircle then extend the straight edge and add a piece to each side as shown by the dotted lines on

4. *Making the sleeve pattern*

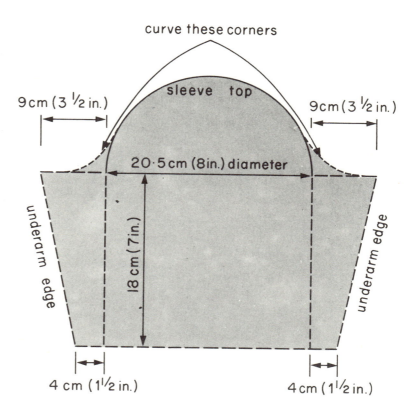

curve these corners

sleeve top

9 cm (3 ½ in.)

9 cm (3 ½ in.)

20·5 cm (8 in.) diameter

underarm edge

underarm edge

18 cm (7 in.)

4 cm (1½ in.)

4 cm (1½ in.)

the diagram. Finally curve the sharp corners at the top part of the sleeves.

Cut two sleeves from velvet and join the underarm edges of each one. Pin the curved top edge of each sleeve 1·3cm ($\frac{1}{2}$ in.) under each shoulder strap then pin the remainder of the top sleeve edge to the inside of the bodice at the underarm. Note that for smaller sizes the sleeves may have to be cut a little smaller all round to fit the armhole size of the bodice. Sew the

sleeves in place as pinned. Stitch the braids to the neck edge of the bodice and straps as illustrated.

Gather the waist edge of the skirt to fit the lower edge of the bodice. Sew the waist edge of the skirt to the lower edge of the bodice. Try the dress on the child and turn up the lower edge to make the skirt floor length. Hem the lower edge. Sew hooks and eyes to the back edges of the dress.

5. *Sewing the cuff seam*

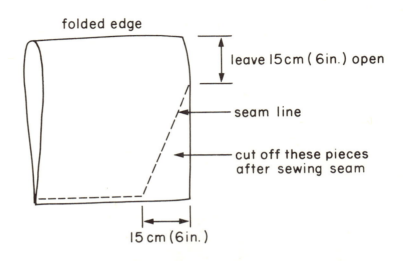

folded edge

leave 15cm (6in.) open

seam line

cut off these pieces
after sewing seam

15 cm (6in.)

To make the brocade under sleeves

Cut two 46cm by 51cm (18 in. by 20 in.) pieces of fabric. Join the 46cm (18 in.) edges of each piece. Hem one remaining raw edge on each sleeve and stitch lace edging to it for the cuff frill. Thread elastic through the hemmed edges to fit the child's wrists.

Put the dress on the child and then try on the brocade sleeves. The upper raw edges should extend about 15cm (6 in.) above the elbows. If the brocade sleeves are too long cut the upper raw edges to fit. Turn in the upper raw edges and gather them to fit the lower edges of the velvet dress sleeves. Lap the gathered edges 1.3cm ($\frac{1}{2}$ in.) over the velvet sleeve edges and slip stitch in place.

To make the turned back cuffs

Cut two 40.5cm by 102cm (16 in. by 40 in.) strips of fur fabric or brocade. Note that for smaller sizes these cuffs should be made proportionately smaller. The illustration gives a guide as to the correct length of the cuffs in relation to the costume.

Fold the cuff pieces in half bringing the 40.5cm (16 in.) edges together then stitch the seam as shown in diagram 5. Trim off the excess pieces as indicated in the diagram. If the cuffs are made from brocade, hem the remaining raw edges. Fur fabric edges do not require hemming.

Put the dress on the child then slip on the cuffs over the sleeves as shown in diagram 6. Sew the narrow

64

6. *Fixing the cuff to the sleeve*

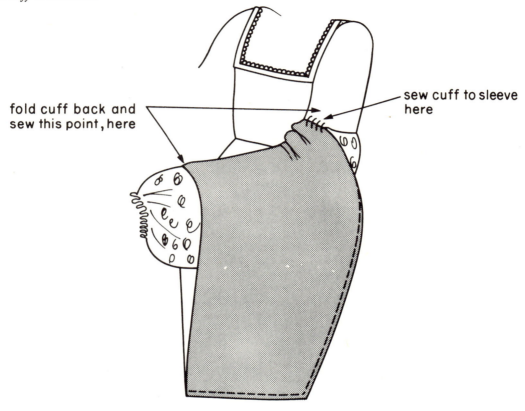

fold cuff back and
sew this point, here

sew cuff to sleeve
here

end of the cuffs to the sleeves as shown in the diagram. Turn the wrist edges of the cuffs right back and catch to the velvet sleeves with a few stitches at the position shown in diagram 6.

Sash

Materials required to fit any size.
46cm ($\frac{1}{2}$ yd) of 92cm (36 in.) wide thin fabric such as nylon chiffon.
2 large beads.
Scraps of narrow braid.

To make

Cut the fabric into two 23cm by 92cm (9 in. by 36 in.) strips. Join them together along one 23cm (9 in.) edge to make one long strip. Join the long raw edges of the strip then turn right side out. Try the sash on the child tying it in a single loop as shown in the illustration. Cut the sash to the correct length if it is too long.

Slip a bead about 13cm (5 in.) inside each end of the sash and tie a thread round the fabric on either side of the bead to hold it in place. Sew a scrap of braid round the fabric on either side of the bead. Hem the raw edges at the ends of the sash.

Gable head-dress

Materials required to fit any size.
A rigid plastic hairband.
A 14cm by 28cm (5½ in. by 11 in.) strip of stiff white card.
70cm (¾ yd) of narrow white tape.
46cm (½ yd) of gold braid or trimming about 1·3cm (½ in.) wide.
58cm (⅝ yd) of 112cm (44 in.) wide thin black fabric for the veil.
A 15cm by 92cm (6 in. by 36 in.) strip of brocade fabric.
Adhesive.

7. *The pattern for the gable head-dress*

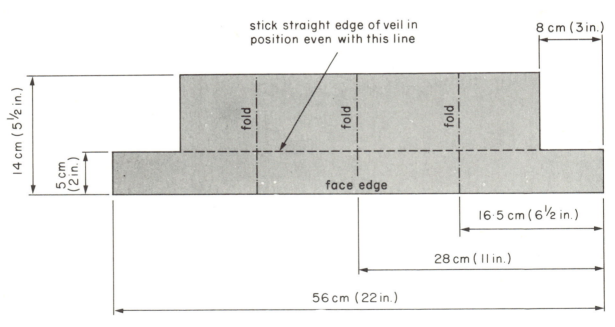

stick straight edge of veil in position even with this line

8 cm (3 in.)

14 cm (5½ in.)

5 cm (2 in.)

fold

fold

fold

face edge

16·5 cm (6½ in.)

28 cm (11 in.)

56 cm (22 in.)

8. *Sticking the hair band inside the gable shape*

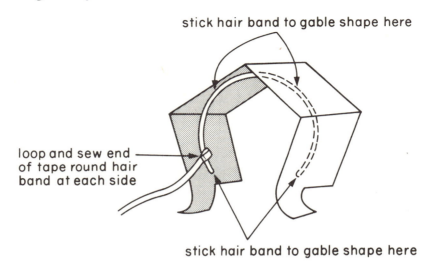

stick hair band to gable shape here

loop and sew end
of tape round hair
band at each side

stick hair band to gable shape here

To make

Cut the card to the shape shown in diagram 7 then fold it along the lines marked 'fold' to make the gable shape. Curl up the extended ends of the gable as shown in diagram 8.

Place the plastic hairband 2·5cm (1 in.) inside the face edge of the gable shape and stick it to the card where it touches at the positions shown in diagram 8. Allow the glue to dry. Cut the tape in two pieces and sew one end of each tape round the hairband at each side as shown in the diagram, for tying under the chin.

For the veil cut a 112cm (44 in.) diameter semicircle of black fabric. Make a 25·5cm (10 in.) cut in the veil as shown in diagram 9 then hem all the raw edges.

Place the straight edge of the veil over the back part of the gable shape and stick in place as indicated in diagram 7 so that the veil will hang down the back.

For the ornamental band, join the long raw edges and across one short end of the strip of brocade fabric. Turn right side out and press then turn in and slip stitch the remaining raw edges. Place the band on the front portion of the gable shape to cover the card having the ends hanging down equally at each side. Stick the band in place but do not stick it to the curled up pieces of card. Fold the long ends of the band back up towards the centre top of the head dress and pin them there. One side of the veil can also be looped up at the back and pinned in this position

67

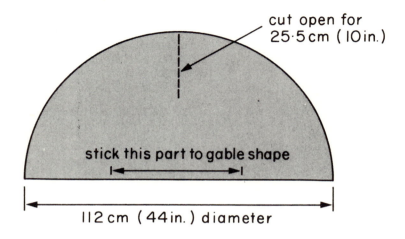

cut open for
25·5 cm (10 in.)

stick this part to gable shape

112 cm (44 in.) diameter

leaving the other side hanging down as shown in the illustration.

Finally stick the braid at right angles to the front edge of the head dress as illustrated, clipping it at the corners to fit.

Underskirt

Make in the same way as given for the Victorian evening dress underskirt.

Hairstyle

The hair should be parted in the centre at the front and pinned up to be hidden by the head dress.

Jewellery

As many finger rings as desired may be worn. Plain beads or strings of pearls can be sewn in loops to the bodice front as shown in the illustration. Thin silky gold cord is used here for the neck 'chains' with a brooch sewn to one of them for a pendant.

Welsh
costume

This costume provides an alternative idea for using the high crowned Puritan hat. A white cap, checked shawl and striped skirt complete the Welsh costume.

Hat, apron and underskirt

Make these in exactly the same way as given in the instructions for the Puritan costume.

Blouse

Use an ordinary long-sleeved white blouse.

Skirt

Materials required to fit any size.
Two strips of 92cm (36 in.) wide blue and white, or black and white, striped fabric; the required waist to floor measurement. Note that the stripes should run parallel to the selve edges of the fabric.
Length of 2·5cm (1 in.) wide petersham ribbon, the child's waist measurement plus 5cm (2 in.) for an overlap.
5cm (2 in.) strip of *Velcro* or hooks and eyes instead.
1·9m (2 yd) of ric-rac or other braid.

To make

Join the strips together at the selve edges leaving a 15cm (6 in.) gap at the top of one seam for the skirt opening. Press the seam to one side. Neaten the cut ends of the ribbon. Gather the waist edge of the skirt to fit the ribbon strip. Lap one long edge of the ribbon over the gathered skirt edge and stitch in place. Sew the *Velcro* or hooks and eyes to the ends of the ribbon where they overlap.

Hem the lower edge then sew the braid about 8cm (3 in.) above the hem edge.

Shawl

Use a 92cm (1 yd) square of fabric frayed out at the raw edges to form fringe. Alternatively a Paisley patterned shawl or scarf can be used if available.

Cap

Materials required to fit any size.
35cm ($\frac{3}{8}$ yd) of 92cm (36 in.) wide white cotton fabric.
1·2m ($1\frac{1}{4}$ yd) of lace edging about 2·5cm (1 in.) wide.
92cm (1 yd) of white tape for ties.
58cm ($\frac{5}{8}$ yd) of narrow elastic.

To make

Cut a 61cm (24 in.) diameter semicircle of fabric. The curved edge of this shape is the face edge of the cap. Turn in the curved edge 1·3cm ($\frac{1}{2}$ in.) and stitch in place forming a casing for the elastic. Stitch lace edging to this curved edge. Thread through a 46cm (18 in.) length of elastic stitching the ends of the elastic securely in place at each end.

Turn in the straight edge 1·3cm ($\frac{1}{2}$ in.) and stitch in place leaving a gap in the stitching at the centre for threading the elastic through. Insert the remainder of the elastic here, stitching the ends in place about 8cm (3 in.) from each end of the cap so that the centre part is gathered up as shown in diagram 1. Slip stitch the gap in the stitching.

Cut the white tape in two pieces and sew one to each side of the cap to tie under the chin.

Hairstyle

The hair should be hidden underneath the cap.

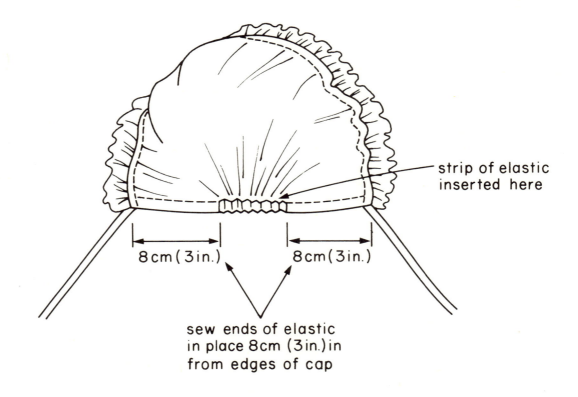

strip of elastic
inserted here

8cm (3in.)   8cm (3in.)

sew ends of elastic
in place 8cm (3in.) in
from edges of cap

1. *Back view of cap showing how elastic is inserted*

Eastern costume

Thin non-fray nylon jersey fabric is used for the costume illustrated here. Nylon chiffon or very fine curtain nets are also suitable. The costume is extremely easy to make.

Pants

Materials required for height 147cm (4 ft 10-in.).
2·1m (2¼ yd) of fabric 122cm (48 in.) or more in width.
46cm (½ yd) of narrow elastic.
A strip of fancy lurex braid about 4cm (1½ in.) wide, the child's hip measurement plus 5cm (2 in.).
2 hooks and eyes.

To make

Cut two pieces of fabric 122cm (48 in.) or more in width by the child's hip to ankle measurement plus 20·5cm (8 in.). Fold each piece in half as shown in diagram 1 and stitch a narrow seam for the inside leg seam leaving 25·5cm (10 in.) open at the top of the seam for the crotch of the pants. Note that for smaller sizes the crotch depth will probably need to be less than 25·5cm (10 in.) and the pants should be tried on the child to find the correct size.

Sew the two leg pieces together at the crotch taking a narrow seam as shown in diagram 2 and leaving a small opening in the top of one seam for the back opening of the pants.

Hem the ankle edges of the pants then thread elastic through each hem to fit the ankles. Gather the top edge of the pants to fit the hips. Neaten the ends of the fancy braid then lap one long edge of the braid over the gathered edge of the pants and stitch in place. Sew hooks and eyes to the ends of the braid at the back overlap.

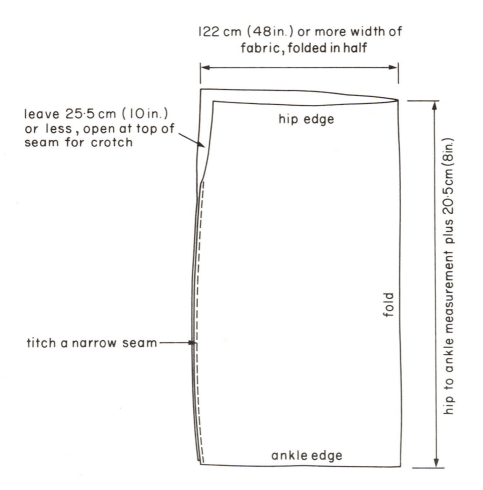

122 cm (48 in.) or more width of
fabric, folded in half

hip edge

leave 25·5 cm (10 in.)
or less, open at top of
seam for crotch

fold

hip to ankle measurement plus 20·5 cm (8 in.)

titch a narrow seam

ankle edge

1. *Stitching the inside leg seam on the pants leg*

2. *Sewing the crotch seams*

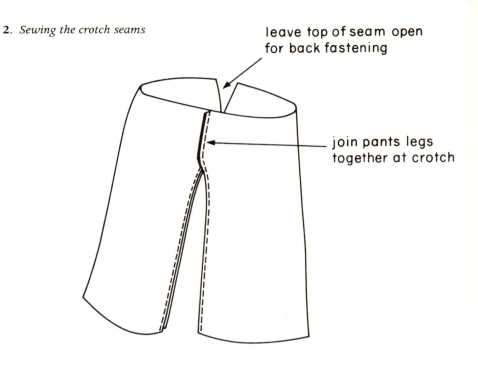

leave top of seam open
for back fastening

join pants legs
together at crotch

Bodice

Materials required for height 147cm (4 ft 10-in.).
35cm ($\frac{3}{8}$ yd) of 92cm (36 in.) wide lurex fabric for
the bodice.
1·6m (1$\frac{3}{4}$ yd) of the same kind of braid as used for
the pants.
35cm ($\frac{3}{8}$ yd) of the same kind of fabric as used for
the pants, for the sleeves.
1·4m (1$\frac{1}{2}$ yd) of narrow braid for edging the sleeves.
4 hooks and eyes.
Oddment of fabric for making a pattern for the
bodice.

3. *Pinning the bodice pattern on the bodice fabric*

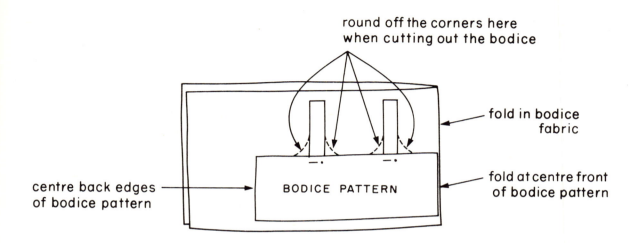

round off the corners here
when cutting out the bodice

fold in bodice
fabric

fold at centre front
of bodice pattern

centre back edges
of bodice pattern

BODICE PATTERN

To make

Make a pattern for the bodice using the oddment of fabric as follows, cut a 15cm (6 in.) wide strip of fabric the child's chest measurement plus 5cm (2 in.). Place it around the child underneath the arms then overlap and pin the back edges to fit. If the strip is too wide, cut it a little narrower. Now cut two 4cm by 30·5cm ($1\frac{1}{2}$ in. by 12 in.) strips of fabric and pin them to the band for shoulder straps shortening the straps as necessary to make them fit neatly.

Take off the bodice pattern and cut across each shoulder strap at the top of the shoulder so that the pattern can be laid flat. Fold the pattern in half having the fold at the centre front. Pin the pattern on to the piece of bodice fabric as shown in diagram 3 placing the fold at a fold in the bodice fabric. Now cut out the bodice rounding off the corners where the straps meet the bodice band as shown by the dotted lines in diagram 3.

Join the shoulder straps of the bodice taking narrow seams. Put the bodice on the child wrong side out and pin a dart in each side to make it fit neatly as shown in diagram 4. Stitch the darts as pinned.

Turn in all the raw edges 0·6cm ($\frac{1}{4}$ in.) and stitch, clipping the curves if necessary. Turn in each centre

4. *Pinning the darts in the bodice*

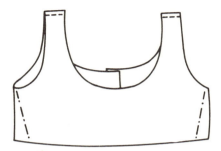

back edge another 0·6cm ($\frac{1}{4}$ in.) and stitch. Sew fancy braid round the neck and lower edges of the bodice then sew the hooks and eyes to the back edges.

For each sleeve cut a 30·5cm by 61cm (12 in. by 24 in.) strip of fabric. Note that the 30·5cm (12 in.) measurement is the length of the sleeves and for smaller sizes the sleeves will need to be cut shorter so that they will be elbow length. Join the 30·5cm (12 in.) edges of each sleeve taking a narrow seam. Sew narrow braid to one long raw edge of each sleeve. Gather the remaining long raw edges to fit the arm-holes of the bodice then sew them in place.

Veil

Materials required to fit any size.
A strip of narrow braid for the headband long enough to go round the child's head plus 2·5cm (1 in.).
70 cm ($\frac{3}{4}$ yd) of the same type of fabric as used for the pants but in a contrasting colour if desired.
An oddment of jewellery such as a pendant or brooch.

To make

Join the end of the braid then sew the piece of jewellery to the band to hang down on the forehead as illustrated.

Sew the centre part of one long edge of the fabric to the band at the centre front and down each side as shown in the illustration.

Sandals

Plastic flip-flop sandals are suitable.

Victorian evening dress, c 1850

This pretty dress is easy to make using bris-bise net curtaining. This type of curtaining is made in widths of between 25·5cm to 35·5cm (10 in. to 14 in.) but alternatively ordinary 122cm (48 in.) wide net curtain fabric can be used cut into narrow strips along the length. The bris-bise used for the dress illustrated is white and has a floral pattern in white and yellow.

A 'crinoline' shape can be achieved by making a very full underskirt using old cotton sheeting or any other available oddments of fabric.

Dress

Materials required for height 147cm (4 ft 10-in.).
17·4m (19 yd) of bris-bise net curtaining 35·5cm (14 in.) in width, note that narrower widths can be used for smaller sizes.

3·5m ($3\frac{3}{4}$ yd) of 92cm (36 in.) wide dress lining fabric such as satin or taffeta, the same colour as the net curtaining.
2·8m (3 yd) of wide ribbon.
46cm ($\frac{1}{2}$ yd) of narrow elastic.
Hooks and eyes for the back fastening.

To make

For the basic skirt cut a 2·8m by 92cm (3 yd by 36 in.) strip of dress lining fabric. The 92cm (36 in.) measurement is the waist to floor length of the skirt, for smaller sizes adjust this measurement accordingly.

Narrowly hem one long edge of the fabric for the hem edge of the skirt. Mark a line on the fabric parallel to the hem edge and 1·3cm ($\frac{1}{2}$ in.) less than the width of the bris-bise away from it as shown in diagram 1. Cut a 5·5m (6 yd) length of bris-bise and

1. *Marking the line for the first frill on the skirt*

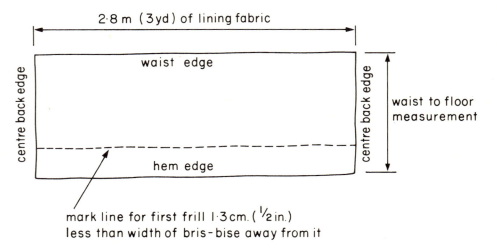

mark line for first frill 1·3cm. ($\frac{1}{2}$ in.) less than width of bris-bise away from it

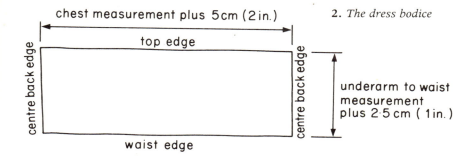

chest measurement plus 5cm (2 in.)

top edge

centre back edge

centre back edge

waist edge

2. *The dress bodice*

underarm to waist
measurement
plus 2·5 cm (1 in.)

3. *Pinning on the shoulder straps and side darts*

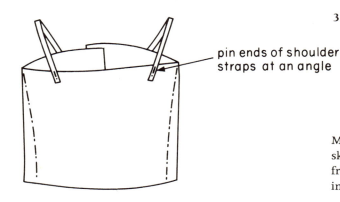

pin ends of shoulder
straps at an angle

gather the top edge to measure 2·8m (3 yd). Sew the gathered edge in place on the skirt along the marked line.

For the top frill cut a 2·8m (3 yd) length of bris-bise. Sew the top edge of this to the top waist edge of the skirt, this edge is gathered up later on forming the frill.

For the middle frill cut a 5·5m (6 yd) length of bris-bise, gather the top edge to measure 2·8m (3 yd).

Mark the position of the top edge of this frill on the skirt between the other two frills taking care that the frills will overlap one another equally. Sew the frill in place.

Join the centre back edges of the skirt leaving a 15cm (6 in.) gap at the top of the seam for the back opening. Press the seam to one side.

For the dress bodice cut two strips of dress lining fabric and one strip of bris-bise to the sizes shown in diagram 2. Having the bris-bise between the two layers of lining fabric join all the edges except for the waist edge. Turn right side out and press then tack the waist edges together. The bris-bise is the right side of the bodice. From the remaining piece of lining fabric cut two 30·5cm by 4cm (12 in. by $1\frac{1}{2}$ in.) strips

81

for the shoulder straps. Turn in the long raw edges, fold the strips in half lengthwise, then stitch, forming narrow straps.

Place the bodice inside out around the child then overlap and pin the back edges to fit. Place a shoulder strap over each shoulder. Pin the ends of the straps to the bodice as shown in diagram 3 shortening them as necessary to make the bodice fit neatly under the arms. Now pin a dart in each side of the bodice

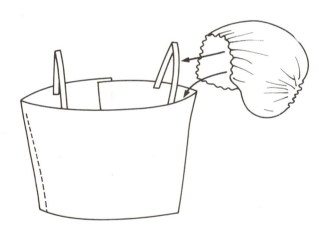

4. *Sewing the sleeve in position*

through all thicknesses of fabric, from the waist edge tapering to the top edge as shown in diagram 3 to make the bodice fit neatly round the waist.

Take off the bodice, stitch the darts as pinned then sew the ends of the straps in place.

For each sleeve cut a 56cm (22 in.) length of bris-bise. Thread a length of elastic through the casing in the top of each piece to fit the child's upper arm. Hold the ends of the elastic in place at each end with a few stitches. Join the short edges of each sleeve piece. Gather up the remaining edges to fit the armhole edges of the bodice. Sew the gathered edges in position on the shoulder straps and underarm of the bodice as shown in diagram 4.

Gather the top edge of the skirt to fit the lower edge of the bodice then sew it in place. Sew hooks and eyes to the centre back overlap of the dress bodice.

For each shoulder piece cut a strip of bris-bise long enough to reach from the back waist edge, over the shoulder to about 8cm (3 in.) below the front waist edge.

Fold each piece along the length about three times to make strips about 13cm (5 in.) in width. Turn in one short end of each strip 1·3cm ($\frac{1}{2}$ in.) and run through a gathering thread pulling up the stitches to gather slightly. Sew these edges in place to the back waist edge of the bodice as shown in diagram 5.

Take the shoulder pieces over the shoulders toward the centre front and catch in place with stitches to the bodice as shown in diagrams 5 and 6. Pleat up the front ends of the shoulder pieces and sew the pleats in place. Sew the ends in place as shown in diagram 6. Sew on a ribbon bow to cover the ends of the shoulder pieces at the centre front leaving loops of ribbon hanging down as illustrated.

catch shoulder pieces to top of
shoulder straps and top of bodice
with a stitch here

5. *Sewing the shoulder pieces in position
at the back*

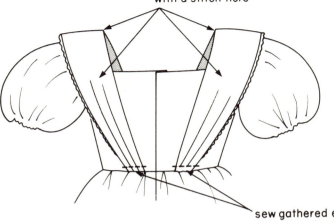

sew gathered ends of
shoulder pieces here at back

catch to bodice with
a stitch here

6. *Sewing the shoulder pieces in position
at the front*

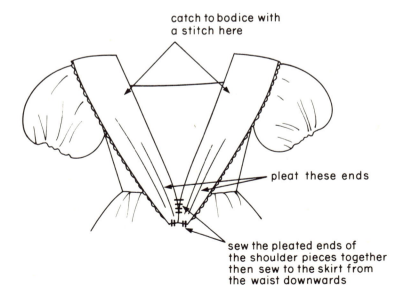

pleat these ends

sew the pleated ends of
the shoulder pieces together
then sew to the skirt from
the waist downwards

83

7. Making a three-tiered underskirt

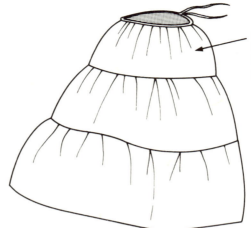

use about 2·8m (3yd)
for the top tier and more
fullness for the second
and third tiers

Underskirt

Make this as full as possible according to the fabric
available. A three-tiered skirt is best as shown in
diagram 7 using 2·8m (3 yd) for the top tier and adding
more fullness to the second and third tiers. The
gathered waist edge can be sewn to a length of tape
leaving enough tape at each end for tying round the
waist.

Hair

If the hair is long it should be pinned up in to a bun
or coiled plaits. Ribbon bows, loops, artificial flowers
are all suitable trimmings for pinning in to the hair.

The Celts wore brightly coloured fabrics woven in checks and stripes making a sort of patchwork effect. The tunic and cloak are very easy to make from rectangles of fabric. Although fur fabric is used for the cloak illustrated, blanket material or plain non-woven curtain fabric could be used instead. The 'jewellery' is made from gold coloured dressing gown cord and buttons.

Tunic

Materials required to fit any size.
A piece of 137cm (54 in.) wide checked or striped fabric which should be the child's shoulder to floor length; note that for a very small child 122cm (48 in.) wide fabric will do instead of 137cm (54 in.).

To make
Fold the fabric in half across the width and cut in to two pieces as shown in diagram 1. Join the pieces together at the sides to within 23cm (9 in.) of the top edges. Join the top edges leaving 28cm (11 in.) open at the centre for the neck as shown in diagram 2.

Turn in the raw edges at the neck and armhole edges and stitch in place. Hem the lower edge.

width of fabric folded in half

shoulder to floor length

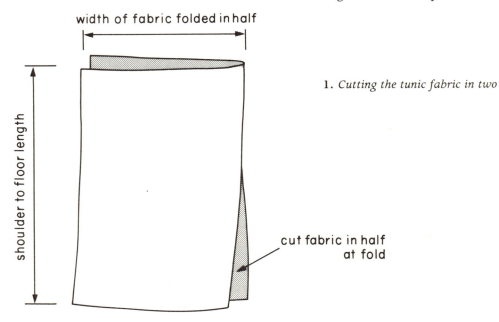

1. *Cutting the tunic fabric in two*

cut fabric in half
at fold

2. Joining the side and shoulder seams of the tunic

28cm (11in.) left open for neck

23 cm (9 in.) left open at each side for armholes

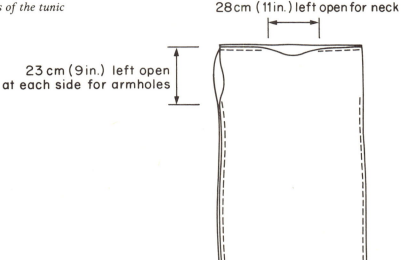

Belt

Use a length of gold braid or ribbon, fastening it at the ends with *Velcro* or hooks and eyes.

Cloak

Materials required to fit any size.
1·2m (1¼ yd) of 137cm (54 in.) wide fabric; note that the width of the fabric is the length of the cloak and therefore for a small child 92cm or 122cm (36 in. or 48 in.) wide fabric may do.
46cm (½ yd) of narrow elastic.

To make

Hem one 1·2m (1¼ yd) edge only, on the fur fabric. If other fabric is used, hem all the raw edges. Thread the elastic through one 1·2m (1¼ yd) edge for the neck edge of the cloak adjusting the length of the elastic to fit. Sew the elastic securely in place at each end.

Brooch, headband and bracelet

Materials
2·1m (2¼ yd) of gold dressing gown cord.
Gold buttons as available.
Thin card.
A hook and eye.
A large safety pin.
Adhesive.

3. *Coiling the cord to make the brooch*

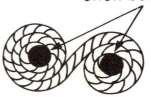

stick buttons here

To make the brooch

Cut a 56cm (22 in.) length of cord and coat the ends with glue to prevent them unravelling. Coil the cord round at each end as shown in diagram 3 using a little glue to hold the coils in place. Stick a circle of card to the back of each coil then attach a safety pin to the back for the fastening. Stick a button to the centre of each coil.

To make the bracelet

Cut a 46cm (18 in.) length of cord and coat the ends with glue as for the brooch. Roll up the ends in the same way as for the brooch leaving enough cord between the coils to go around the arm. Stick card circles to the back of the coils and buttons in the centres. Sew on a hook and eye so that the bracelet can be fastened around the arm.

To make the headband

Coil up the ends of the remaining piece of cord leaving enough cord between the coils to fit around the child's head as shown in the illustration. Glue on card circles and buttons as for the bracelet then sew the coiled ends together.

88

Empire
costume,
c 1815

The very high waistline of this costume is characteristic of the period from about 1790 to 1820. Little short jackets called 'spencers' were worn and these just covered the dress bodices.

For this outfit a plain long sleeved T-shirt is used for the spencer and the dress skirt is attached to it. Spotted white curtain net with frilled edges is used for the skirt but white or pastel coloured cotton fabric with a small printed pattern would also be suitable. The pretty bonnet is covered in fawn fabric to look like straw and decorated with pink ribbons to match the spots on the dress.

Spencer

Use a long sleeved, high necked T-shirt or sweater in a dark colour.

Skirt, wrist and neck frills, puffed sleeves

Materials required for height 147cm (4 ft 10 in.).
1·9m (2 yd) of frilled edged curtain net 102cm (40 in.) or more in width for the skirt.
The same amount of cotton or lining fabric for lining the skirt.
2·3m (2½ yd) of 2·5cm (1 in.) wide ribbon for the skirt band, wrist and neck bands and sleeve bands.
33cm (13 in.) of *Velcro*.
58cm (⅝ yd) of 92cm (36 in.) wide fabric to match the T-shirt, for the puffed sleeves.

To make the skirt

First cut the frill off one edge of the skirt fabric and sew it in position about 15cm (6 in.) above the frill on the opposite edge. This double frilled edge will be the hem edge of the skirt and it can be

1. Cutting the skirt to the correct length

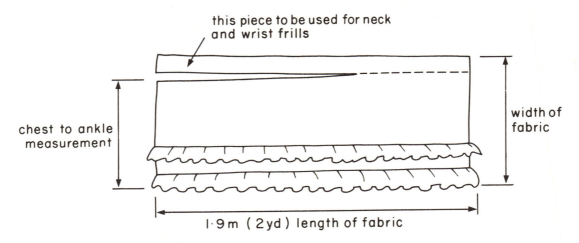

this piece to be used for neck
and wrist frills

chest to ankle
measurement

width of
fabric

1·9 m (2 yd) length of fabric

decorated if desired with more frills and ruffles of ribbon.

Measure the correct skirt length on the child taking the measurement from the chest to just above the ankles. Trim a piece off the top edge of the skirt to make the skirt the correct length as shown in diagram 1.

Join the short edges of the skirt piece leaving 15cm (6 in.) open at the top of the seam for the centre back opening of the skirt. Press the seam to one side.

Make the skirt lining in the same way as the skirt omitting the frills and hemming the lower edge. Place the lining inside the skirt and tack the top raw edges together.

Cut a strip of ribbon long enough to go round the child's chest plus 5cm (2 in.) for an overlap. Neaten the cut ends of the ribbon. Gather the top raw edges of the skirt to fit the ribbon strip noting that about

25·5cm (10 in.) should be left ungathered at the centre front of the skirt. Lap one long edge of the ribbon over the gathered top edges of the skirt and stitch in place. Sew 5cm (2 in.) strips of *Velcro* to the ends of the ribbon where they overlap.

To make the skirt stay in the required high waisted position, strips of *Velcro* are sewn to the ribbon band and to the T-shirt. The *Velcro* strips can be removed if the T-shirt is to be used for ordinary wear later on.

Place the skirt on the child in the correct position on top of the T-shirt then mark the position of the top edge of the ribbon band on the T-shirt at the centre front, under the arms and at each side at the back. Take off the T-shirt and sew on 4cm (1½ in.) strips of the furry side of the *Velcro* at the marked positions. Sew the corresponding hooked strips of *Velcro* inside the ribbon band of the skirt at the centre front, sides and back.

91

To make the wrist and neck frills

Cut strips of ribbon long enough to go round the neck and each wrist on top of the T-shirt allowing 5cm (2 in.) extra on each strip for neatening the ends of the ribbon and an overlap. Gather up narrow strips of the remaining skirt fabric and sew to the ribbon strips. Sew on 2·5cm (1 in.) strips of *Velcro* at the overlaps.

To Make the puffed sleeves

Make a pattern for the sleeves by drawing out a 51cm (20 in.) diameter semicircle. Using this pattern cut two sleeves from fabric. Cut two strips of ribbon long enough to go round the child's upper arm plus 2·5cm (1 in.), for the sleeve bands.

Gather the straight edges of the sleeves to fit the ribbon bands then lap one long edge of each band over the gathered edge of the sleeve and sew it in place.

Fold each sleeve in half bringing the ends of the ribbon bands together and join the raw edges of bands and sleeves for 8cm (3 in.) as shown in diagram 2.

Turn the sleeves right side out and gather up the remaining raw edges to fit the armhole edges of the T-shirt. Slip each puffed sleeve over the T-shirt sleeves, turn in the gathered raw edges and slip stitch the sleeves in position. The puffed sleeves can be removed if the T-shirt is to be used for ordinary wear later on.

Bonnet

Materials required to fit any size.
46cm ($\frac{1}{2}$ yd) of 82cm (32 in.) wide stiff interlining for the bonnet shape.
70cm ($\frac{3}{4}$ yd) of 92cm (36 in.) wide thin curtain net or cotton fabric for covering the bonnet shape.

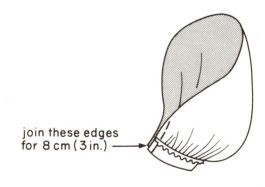

join these edges
for 8 cm (3 in.) ──▶

2. Joining the sleeve seam

92

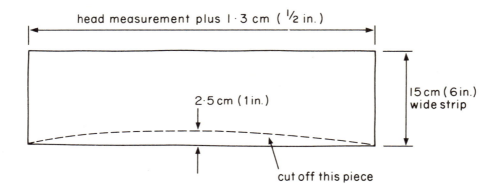

head measurement plus 1·3 cm (½ in.)

15 cm (6 in.)
wide strip

2·5 cm (1 in.)

cut off this piece

3. *Cutting a curved piece off one edge of the bonnet strip*

Trimmings for the bonnet as available, ribbons or strips of curtain net, rosettes, artificial flowers, feathers etc.
1·6m (1¾ yd) bias binding to match the bonnet fabric.
Adhesive.

To make

Cut a 15cm (6 in.) wide strip of interlining long enough to go round the child's head plus 1·3cm (½ in.). Cut one long edge of this strip in to a curved shape as shown in diagram 3. Overlap the 15cm (6 in.) edges of the strip 1·3cm (½ in.) and glue or sew in place forming a tube. The overlap will be at the centre back of the bonnet.

For the bonnet brim cut a 30·5cm (12 in.) diameter circle of interlining. Place the cut curved edge of the tube on to the bonnet brim a little off centre as shown

4. *Placing the crown of the bonnet on the brim*

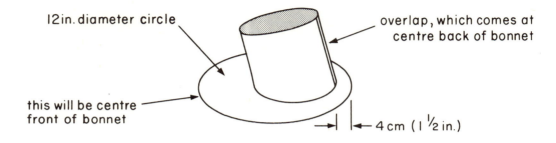

12in. diameter circle

overlap, which comes at
centre back of bonnet

this will be centre
front of bonnet

4 cm (1 ½ in.)

in diagram 4. Mark the shape of the tube on to the bonnet brim. Carefully cut out the marked circle then place this small circle on to the top of the tube for the top of the bonnet. Oversew the edges of the tube and circle together as shown in diagram 5. This forms the completed crown of the bonnet.

To cover the bonnet crown, cut a 48·5cm (19 in.) diameter circle of bonnet fabric. Run a gathering thread round the edge and place the circle over the bonnet crown pulling up the gathers to fit inside the lower edge of the tube. Oversew the fabric to the tube at the lower edge.

To cover the brim of the bonnet, spread a little adhesive round the outer and inner edges of the brim shape then stick it on to a piece of the bonnet fabric. Cut out the fabric even with the interlining shape. Cover the other side of the brim with fabric in the

5. *Sewing the small circle to the top of the tube*

same way. Bind the outer and inner edges of the brim with bias binding.

Place the bonnet crown in position on the brim as shown in diagram 4 and oversew the inner edge of the brim to the lower edge of the tube.

Attach a length of ribbon across the top of the bonnet slightly toward the back so that the hat can be tied on under the chin bending down the brim at each side as shown in the illustration.

Trim the bonnet as desired. The bonnet illustrated has a ruffle of ribbon sewn to the inside edge of the brim. Strips of ribbon and net fabric are wound round the crown and made in to rosettes and a few feathers are sewn on.

Socks and gloves

These can be white or pastel coloured.

Shoes

Use flat slippers or ballet shoes with a small ribbon bow sewn to the front of each one.

Hairstyle

Short hair can be formed in to little ringlets on the forehead and the back will be hidden by the bonnet. Long hair should be parted in the centre and pinned in a bun on top of the head which will fit inside the crown of the bonnet.